ONE WOMAN SHOW

MONOLOGUES
AS ORIGINALLY WRITTEN
AND PERFORMED BY

CORNELIA OTIS SKINNER

THE DRAMATIC PUBLISHING COMPANY

*** NOTICE ***

The amateur and stock acting rights to this work are controlled exclusively by THE DRAMATIC PUBLISHING COMPANY without whose permission in writing no performance of it may be given. Royalty fees are given in our current catalogue and are subject to change without notice. Royalty must be paid every time a play is performed whether or not it is presented for profit and whether or not admission is charged. A play is performed anytime it is acted before an audience. All inquiries concerning amateur and stock rights should be addressed to:

DRAMATIC PUBLISHING
P. O. Box 129, Woodstock, Illinois 60098.

COPYRIGHT LAW GIVES THE AUTHOR OR THE AUTHOR'S AGENT THE EXCLUSIVE RIGHT TO MAKE COPIES. This law provides authors with a fair return for their creative efforts. Authors earn their living from the royalties they receive from book sales and from the performance of their work. Conscientious observance of copyright law is not only ethical, it encourages authors to continue their creative work. This work is fully protected by copyright. No alterations, deletions or substitutions may be made in the work without the prior written consent of the publisher. No part of this work may be reproduced or transmitted in any form or by any means, electronic or mechanical, including photocopy, recording, videotape, film, or any information storage and retrieval system, without permission in writing from the publisher. It may not be performed either by professionals or amateurs without payment of royalty. All rights, including but not limited to the professional, motion picture, radio, television, videotape, foreign language, tabloid, recitation, lecturing, publication, and reading are reserved. *On all programs this notice should appear:*

"Produced by special arrangement with
THE DRAMATIC PUBLISHING COMPANY of Woodstock, Illinois"

©MCMLXXIV by
CORNELIA OTIS SKINNER

Printed in the United States of America
All Rights Reserved
(ONE WOMAN SHOW)

ISBN 0-87129-464-8

CONTENTS

Preface	
Christmas Morning	1
A Box of Powder	9
Hotel Porch	16
Being Presented	23
Homework	30
A Lady Explorer	37
Monte Carlo	43
The Facts of Life	49
Motoring in the 90's	57
Sailing Time	64
American Ancestor Worship	69
Ancestor Worship East	69
Ancestor Worship West	73
Ancestor Worship North	76
Ancestor Worship South	79
The Vanishing Red Man	85
A Subscriber to the Symphony	93
The Yearly American Invasion	101
The Shopper	102
The Debutante	104
The Gourmet	105
The Art Student	107
The Correspondent	109
The Lovers	112
The American Wife	113
Minute Man's Wife	116
Appendix	122

PREFACE

The following comprises a collection of my monologues. Monologues, character sketches --call them what you will, as long as nobody uses the absurdly erroneous word "readings." They are printed exactly as I wrote them with myself in mind as solo performer.

Each sketch, of course, is in the form of a one-sided dialogue. The remarks or replies of the other person or persons being implied and indicated by an appropriate pause marked ... / ... The number of dots suggests the time shadings of the pause. If in the action a door is supposed to close or a bell to ring, the words (Door) or (Bell) appear as mere indications of the performer's reaction. There are no off-stage sound effects unless specifically indicated.

Although a program of monologues could certainly come under the heading of "platform performance", I have always tried to create the illusion of real theatre making each performance a "one-woman show."

The ideal setting is a bare stage covered by an unobtrusive rug and backed by plain, neutral-colored curtains. The only furniture should be a small table--lightweight enough for the performer to move about, yet sturdy enough to sit on at required moments--and two chairs, one straight like a dining-room chair, the other with arms but not heavy or upholstered as these, like the table, have occasionally to be shoved around. One word of advice--avoid any clutter in the way of plants. They merely serve to distract. The attention of the audience should be centered on the performer.

Before each number I have indicated the sort of character to be portrayed, together with any essential props. I have also added the brief introductions I used.

A word of encouragement to anyone embarking on these solo flights. Good luck! And if the prospect of finding yourself all alone out there on the stage frightens you, bear in mind the comforting fact that no other actor can steal a scene from you!

CHRISTMAS MORNING

This sketch is self-explanatory and needs no hand props. It presents an average young mother, harassed, but trying to control her two small children and keep her husband on an even keel as they open their Christmas presents.

Introduction

This sketch which is called CHRISTMAS MORNING is a scene in the living room of an average family on that special day. The telephone is indicated by a gesture.

NO, BETSEY DEAR, IT'S SONNY'S TURN! Daddy, will you give Sonny his next present?./. I wonder what it can be! Oh Frank, dear, he wants to open it himself! Yes, Betsey, just as soon as Sonny opens his. Oh, help him, Frank, he's getting all caught up in the string. Want Daddy to help you, dear? . . / . . Maybe you'd better not, Frank . . No, Betsey, don't go prying into the other packages, you wait!.. Who's it from, Frank? ./. Well now, what do you suppose Uncle Albert's sent you, Sonny? Let's all guess ../.. (LOOKING AT PACKAGE.) Oh, Sonny, how perfectly lovely! Just what is it? It's something

Page 2 ONE WOMAN SHOW

mechanical...A steam engine?...Isn't it fascinating!
Well it has to be put together...Daddy'll help you
put it together..Won't you, Frank?../.. Yes now,
why not?../.. Well, the child wants it...it's Christmas..Oh here, Frank. Something for you from
Clara../..Not now, -- after you've fixed Sonny's
steam engine. Now then, Betsey, here's the next
present for you../.. Oh Betsey, how perfectly
lovely! *Another* box of paints! I don't believe any
little girl ever got so many boxes of paints!
(LOOKING AT CARD) From Aunt Lou! Well,
now wasn't that lovely of Aunt Lou../..What,
Sonny?../..Daddy's putting up your steam engine.
After he puts it up you can play with it. Here,
come get this present for *you* from Aunt Lou!
Frank, I think that was a little shabby of Lou.
She could have sent more of a present...And what's
Sonny got? Why Sonny, another box of paints!
No, Betsey, don't grab his paints...They're just
exactly like yours. Betsey, let go, dear!....Sonny,
if you kick her I'll spank you! Now Children, is
that any way to act on Christmas morning?
Betsey, before you get a single present, you pick
up every one of those paints! Don't put them
near your mouth.../.. Mother uses lip-stick --
that's very different...What, Frank?../..Oh have they

ONE WOMAN SHOW   Page 3

gone out, dear? Now you see Children, what
happens when you fight that way? You've pulled
the plug and all the lights are out on the tree.
Will you fix them, Frank?../..No, not right away -
after you've done that../..Well, Frank, they didn't
mean to../..I know, dear, but it's Christmas, they
are excited...Well, I'll put it back in. No, don't you
move. (GETTING TO HANDS AND KNEES.)
I'll do it. Which one is it, Frank?...Frank, you don't
need to get up - just tell me which plug it is. Never
mind - I've got it, now, Sonny, please get away../..
No, you can't help me at all..get away! Now my
dress is caught on the tree. Betsey, unfasten me
will you?../..I'm caught../..I don't know but I'm
caught. Will someone help me or are you going to
leave me here all morning?../..It's the back of my
dress, Frank../..I don't know, one of the trimmings.
If I stand up I'll pull the whole tree over...Oh,
Frank, you don't have to put on your glasses for
that. Just uncatch whatever it is....There! (GET-
TING OUT.) Now, you see, that was simple
enough. Here, Betsey, from Cousin Clara. Oh,
Dora, last night's mail? Thanks. (START OPEN-
ING.) More Christmas cards. Sonny, what on
earth are you doing in the fireplace?../ .Well, he's
not up there - he went back to Alaska or Green-
land - wherever he lives - you're getting all sooty.

ONE WOMAN SHOW

Sonny, come *out* of there! Here's a card from the
Nolans, Frank. A nice picture of their horses...
"Yuletide Greetings from the Nolans." What did
Cousin Clara send you, Betsey?../..A muffler? Isn't
that lovely?../..Why it *is* lovely, Betsey..you're getting
very spoiled. And here's one from Lib and
Harry. "Noel, Noel," it says... Look! It's their
new house in Kansas City. I'm showing you. This
is from Mrs. Jackson. Not very original...just
three men and a star. Here, Betts, put these in the
basket - not the wastebasket! The one for the
Christmas cards! Ha! "Peace on Earth and Good
Will to Men," from the home laundry! Sonny keep
out of Daddy's way while he's putting your toy
together../..He'll be through in a minute../..Of
course he'll let you play with it. - That's what he's
putting it together for. Frank, you and I got a
beautiful Stilton cheese and I've lost the card that
came with it. Betsey, you've just got to stop
throwing paper around...things get lost. Frank did
you see the card that came with this cheese?../..I
merely asked if you saw../..Well, you can do that
and answer too can't you? I don't see what you're
so cross about../..Oh Betsey, what a perfectly
charming doll! Who's it from?../..Didn't it have
a card with it?../..It must have..Where did you unwrap
it?../..It must have had a card with it../..

ONE WOMAN SHOW   Page 5

Which is the paper? Frank, hand me that piece of
paper over there..just that piece...Frank, what's the
matter with you? Please, dear, that toy of Sonny's
can wait a minute. Betsey's got a very fine doll
and she's lost the card that was with it../..There
must have been a card, Betsey../..Because there always *is* a card../..Well, Santa Claus didn't give you
that../..Because I know. It's too expensive../..I
don't know if Santa Claus is rich../..Oh, Betsey,
don't ask so many questions, help me look for the
card and don't mess things up../..Sonny, didn't you
hear Daddy say not to bother him while he's fixing your toy. No, he's not. He says you're playing with his steam engine, Frank../..Daddy's just
seeing if it works. No, Betsey, that's not for you,
don't open it../..It's for Daddy.../..Because I can
tell from the shape..it's a bottle. Let it alone.
(PHONE RINGS) I'll go. That's going to be some
of the family../..I'll go, Dora. Now children, don't
touch anything while mother's talking on the
phone. Hello? Hello? Hello there, Sue. It's Sue,
Frank. Merry Christmas! How are you all?../..
Yes, we're having ours, are you having yours?../..
Just lovely. We haven't opened all our presents
yet. (HAND OVER RECEIVER.) Frank, it's Sue.
What did she send us?../..Well, *think!*../..I said we
hadn't opened all our presents yet so../..Oh did you

like them? I'm so glad../..Want to speak to Frank?
../..Frank, Sue wants to say Merry Christmas to
you../..(SLAPPING HAND OVER MOUTHPIECE.)
Oh come along Frank!..Frank's fixing a mechanical toy of Sonny's. He's working on it as if he
were Edison. Wait, here's Sonny, he wants to
speak to you../..Yes, you do too, Sonny. Come
along now, speak to Aunt Sue../..Just say Merry
Christmas../..Sonny! Come on, now. And thank
her for the lovely present she sent you../..I don't
remember, but she must have sent you something
so be sure and thank her. (SONNY TALKS
BRIEFLY.) I think you might speak to Sue,
Frank. She's calling from all the way out in
Jersey../..All right, but I think it's kind of mean.
(TAKES RECEIVER.) Hello, here I am again..
Oh it's Lloyd! Merry Christmas Lloyd! It's
Lloyd, Frank. Frank says Merry Christmas, Lloyd
../..You do too!...How are you all?../..Just fine../
..Oh having a lovely one../..They did?..At six this
morning?..The children brought their stockings in
to Sue and Lloyd at six this morning. You must
be pretty tired. Want to speak to Betsey? Here,
Betsey, speak to your Uncle Lloyd...Yes, Betsey,
I want you to...He sent you that toy grocery-store
../..Well, he didn't know you had one already.
Betsey, if you don't wish your Uncle Lloyd a

ONE WOMAN SHOW   Page 7

Merry Christmas I'll spank you...Just a minute,
Lloyd, she's coming...(BETSEY SCREAMS.) Betsey
don't scream like, that he'll hear it!...I'm so sorry,
Lloyd. She's just bumped her head../..Yes, that's
she you hear. But I know she thanks you all the
same. Well, Merry Christmas! And tell the children Merry Christmas for us all. Don't eat too
much plum pudding. Merry Christmas! (HANGS
UP.) Betsey, I'm really very cross with you. I
must say, Frank, you didn't set Betsey a very good
example../..Busy?..On that toy, but you've got it
working, haven't you? What's more Sonny wants
to play with it. Sonny, you go right ahead and
play with your steam engine../..I'm not interfering,
Frank. I think the child has a right to his own toy.
It's the one thing he's crazy about...See there,
you've made him cry!../..It does work right. You
know it works perfectly. You're just so childish
you want to play with it yourself. Frank, how can
you talk to me like that before the children. Betsey
keep away...Don't push her, Sonny! Don't hit him,
Betsey. (CHILDREN FIGHT.) Children! Stop it!
Stop it! Stop it! Is that any way to behave on
Christmas. Frank, won't you say something to
them?../..Oh Frank! "Merry Christmas"..what a
thing to say! Well, I can't stand this any more,
I'm going up to get ready for church. Here, I'll

turn on the radio...It may help drown out the noise. (HEARING STRAINS OF "HARK THE HERALD ANGELS SING".) Listen to that. "Peace on Earth and Mercy Mild." I'd just like to know where?

- - - - - - - - -

A BOX OF POWDER

This multiple-character sketch takes place in a well-known beauty salon I call, not too subtly, Dorothy Varden. The speaker indicated as THE SHOPPER is the performer herself. She speaks naturally and leaves characterizations to the other types she subsequently impersonates. There are no hand props.

Introduction

This sketch entitled A BOX OF POWDER takes place in a well-known beauty salon on Fifth Avenue, or in any large city.

THE SHOPPER

MARGIE, I ADORED LUNCHING WITH YOU, and, dear, I think I'll say goodbye because we're right outside Dorothy Varden's../...Mercy, no! I never go in for anything like that. I'm just dropping by to get a box of powder. I know you've got to run. Goodbye, dear, see you soon. (CROSS STAGE.) Good afternoon. I want a box of powder.../..just your regular powder../..: You have no regular powder? I mean your face powder. It comes in a little square blue box.../...

sifted through silk?.../....Oh, I don't think I have to have it sifted through silk. I just want your plain ordinary FACE POWDER. Of course, ha, ha, I know yours isn't ordinary. That's why I buy it.../ ...Well, I don't know the name of the shade exactly. I think it's just sort of medium--not too dark, not too light, just sort of medium.../...*Simonetta.* Is that your medium name? Ha, ha, I mean.../...Well, I don't think I seem exactly like an *Angelica.* Maybe if you'd just let me look at the shades../... Thank you very much; I don't think I need a complexion analysis. I.../...Miss Honeywell? Why that's awfully nice but I haven't got much time; if you'd just.../...

HIGH PRESSURE SALESWOMAN

But Miss Honeywell happens to be in the shop today and will be delighted to give you our three-minute complexion analysis quite free of charge... /...But it won't take any more time and while Miss Honeywell is here it would be a pity to miss the opportunity of having a little chat with her... /...because you see, her advice would be far better than mine. What I mean is *if* you've been using *Simonetta* when what really suits you is *Angelica*

ONE WOMAN SHOW

she could tell at a glance, you see, and who knows, when all's said and done, Madame's need in the long run may turn out to be *Tropicana* or our sensational new *Peach Petal.* I do insist upon Miss Honeywell taking your order because you see our facial contour department is right over here and if Madame would step this way half a mo'--Miss Honeywell! This customer is frightfully keen on having one of your three-minute complexion analyses...

THE SHOPPER

Ha! I'm really not--I mean to say it's awfully nice and I wish I had the time. She didn't get me exactly. What I want is one of those little square blue boxes of powder. It doesn't have to be the kind that's sifted through silk. I think the shade was.../...Thank you very much. I don't need any nourishing cream. The color of the powder was... /...Tissue preservative oil? Thank you, no, I don't preserve my tissues. I think the shade of that powder was.../...Summer cloud cream? No, I don't need any Summer cloud cream. No, I don't need any summer cloud cream. I think the shade of that powder was--would it be *Simonetta*?.../...

Page 12　　　ONE WOMAN SHOW

MISS HONEYWELL
(Seated at table. She is very elegant and and affected.)

Oh, no, my dear, *Simonetta* is definitely the shade for your ash blonde with that creamy pearly pigmentation, and to be quite candid, your skin has definitely a rather yellow cast. You couldn't stand anything lighter than *Morocco Rose,* but let's face it, it won't do a thing for you unless you use it in conjunction with our morn' to midnight finishing foundation. And how is your supply of our hormone enriched cleansing cream?.../... You don't? Then do you mind telling me how you do cleanse your face?.../...You cleanse your face with soap and water! Soap and water? Oh, my dear, my dear, my dear! Well, of course it's your face, but if you'd just let us have it for one course of our herbal contouration treatments, you'd be so gratified. They impart such youthifying vitality and take away all that tired, sallow, crepey look. How long since you have done our figure moulding exercises? My dear, there's never been anything like them for taking away those distressing, ha, ha, well, of course, we in Dorothy Varden's call them the bumps, but let's face it, they are deposits of fatty tissue and they are as stubborn as

ONE WOMAN SHOW   Page 13

they can be unless you get after them the Dorothy Varden way! Now, our Miss Armstrong here is a wizard and she could give you the tip to toe figure analysis and tell you exactly how.../...

THE SHOPPER

I'm sure she could, but I have a pretty good idea of my own figure. By that I don't mean I think my figure is particularly good. If I could just get a box of that powder. I'll take the kind you said I should--that yellow for sallow complexions.../... Miss Armstrong? I'm sure she could, but I haven't got.../...I know, but.../...but.../...Well, isn't the exercise department way up on another floor?.../... Oh, she does happen to be? That's certainly a coincidence, isn't it.../...Miss Armstrong? How do you do?

MISS ARMSTRONG
(The bouncy, energetic type)

Good afternoon! Well, what's our little trouble-- humph, it's not so little, either, is it?.../...I certainly do, Miss Honeywell! I could work wonders with her. Oh, she's not beyond recall. Now, don't you let anybody tell you you're a hopeless case because you're not hopeless at all! See that? See that?

Page 14   ONE WOMAN SHOW

(GESTURE OF PATTING STOMACH.) Regular little hot water bottle, isn't it? Now, my exercises will take that down, augmented, of course, with deep massage. Now, our Miss Svenson here is very, very wonderful on stomachs. She's a fine fanny worker too. I think she'd better take a look at you.../... It's what she's here for.../...Oh, it won't take her a second. Miss Svenson! Do you have a minute? This customer is very interested in one of our exercise courses.

THE SHOPPER
But I'm not!!! I know. I'm overweight, but that's because it's summer and I've been eating. I eat in summer. If someone would just get me a box of that square blue powder, I would.../...

MISS SVENSON
(Speaks with marked Scandinavian accent.)
Oh, yes, I see; She's very large in the buttocks; I think she's got a tendency to double chin. I could take her Thursday at three o'clock. Until then, Madame, go on a diet--no sugar, no starches, no alcohol. See you Thursday at three o'clock.

ONE WOMAN SHOW   Page 15

THE SHOPPER
(In retreat.)

But I didn't say --- never mind, I'll.../...

FRENCH SALESWOMAN
(Complete with gestures.)

Bon jour, Madame. We have just received from Paris a new shipment of evening bags, and so very, very reasonable. Figurez-vous, seventy-five dollars for a brocade evening bag, or maybe Madame would be interested in some French lingerie.../...?

THE SHOPPER
(In full retreat.)

No. No. I was interested in - - - never mind, I'll get it at the drugstore.

- - - - - - - -

HOTEL PORCH

An impersonation of a selfish, wicked old woman who for years has been coming to the same summer resort, preempts the place and makes miserable everybody, especially her daughter, Sarah, now middle-aged. She is best portrayed wearing a woolen shawl and a black velvet ribbon tied about her throat. She sits in an armchair in the middle of the stage. Her voice is somewhat quavery and her accent definitely New England.

Introduction

The setting for this monologue is the wide porch of a New England summer resort hotel. A domineering mother is speaking to her middle-aged daughter.

SARAH. SARAH, YOU'VE GOT MY CHAIR IN THE SUN AGAIN! You know I can't stand the least little bit of sun. Move it back...'Bout two inches further...There. Seems to me that after coming to this hotel for 25 years you ought to be able to tell where I want my chair./.I know, but it does make me so upset. Where's my knitting?./.You did so know I was going to knit, Sarah. I said last night at supper if I don't get

ONE WOMAN SHOW   Page 17

one of my headaches tomorrow I think I'll knit.
And I know you heard me because you said something about winding a new ball of yarn .. don't you remember that, Sarah?./.Well, go on upstairs and get it, then. I shouldn't be surprised if I had one of my headaches after all./.No, I don't want any aspirin. If I get a headache later I'll send you up for them...Good-morning, Mrs. Parker../..Well, as good as can be expected. Those Ormsby boys got in at two o'clock this morning. Made the most infernal racket right underneath my window. I was going to speak to Mr. Tucker about it but then I remembered your daughter was with them ../..Yes, she was with them../..Oh, well, I wouldn't do anything about it. I expect I'm just not used to young people any more../..Oh, Mrs. Parker ... what do you think of the new arrival? Very smart? Well, She struck me as being a bit flashy ../..good-looking though. I wonder what she's doing in a little hotel like this? ... Well, I didn't know if you'd noticed her. I saw Mr. Parker watching her during dinner. I expect she's the kind that attracts the men. There's Mr. Parker waiting for you now ... Hope you enjoy your swim. I hear the jellyfish are rather bad../..Oh, Good morning, Miss Eaton, good morning../..
My daughter? She's gone upstairs to get my

ONE WOMAN SHOW

knitting. Anything I can tell her../..Bridge? This afternoon? Oh, I'm afraid she can't. She's promised to take tea with a friend in North Cabot. She'll be very disappointed, I'm sure. Oh, Miss Eaton. What do you think of this New Yorky looking woman's just arrived?../..You were thinking of asking her to make a fourth at bridge? You must be crazy! I can tell you right here and now that woman plays cards for money. You have only to look at her diamond wristwatch and her painted toenails../.. Oh, well, do what you like but I wouldn't ask her. Well, I'll give Sarah your message. She'll be very disappointed, I know../..Yes, very devoted. Waits on me hand and foot../..Good day, Miss Eaton../.. Good morning, Mr. Tucker. Boston papers late again? I don't like to say anything but that boy you sent down to the station's an awful dawdler.. /..I see you've got a new guest in the hotel../.. What's she doing here?./.Hope you're not going to turn this hotel into a rest-cure for women like that../..She attracts too much attention, Mr. Tucker. What's her name, anyway../..Oh! Originally from Washington?../..She and her husband have just been getting a divorce, haven't they? I suppose she's here resting up a bit before she looks around for a new one. Oh, there you are, Sarah. What took you so long?../..Mail? Any for me?../..

ONE WOMAN SHOW   Page 19

Who's your letter from?../..Well, open it and let's see../..Who did the maid say was asking for you? Miss Eaton? Well, she couldn't have wanted anything very important. I saw her on her way to the beach just now and she didn't say anything about wanting to see you. Have you got my knitting?../.. (GESTURE OF TAKING OUT WORK. THEN PANTOMIME OF KNITTING.) Good morning, Mrs. Cameron../..You going down to the church?../..I thought I might come along and help you with the flowers../..My daughter'd love to help you../.. wouldn't you, Sarah. Oh, Mrs. Cameron. What do you think of the new arrival? ... I don't imagine she'll be in Dr. Cameron's congregation tomorrow. Well, she doesn't look like much of a church-goer to me, and... I don't like to say anything .. but ... she's got number 26 ... right across the hall from me. This morning she went out early for golf ... her door was ajar and I couldn't help but see in ... Mrs. Cameron, there was a bottle of sherry right spang on her bureau. Now, I'm the last person in the world to cause any unpleasantness but I don't think this hotel is a place for a woman traveling alone with a bottle of sherry! Well, I thought maybe you'd say a word to Dr. Cameron and he'd speak to Mr. Tucker about it ... There! How's that, Sarah?../..You think the new woman's very

Page 20 ONE WOMAN SHOW

pretty? ...She's too pretty! This is no place for
her ... What's more she's being served in the dining-
room ahead of me and I won't have her here! Who's
your letter from?../..Mary Pinkney? What's she got
to say?../..Martha's Vineyard? Humph! I suppose
this place isn't grand enough for her../..She wants
what?./.You to come visit her?../..Mary Pinkney
must have lost her mind../..How's that?../..You'd
like to go?../..How long does she ask you for?../..
Three days! I don't suppose it matters what happens to me during those three days. Just means
I'll have to stay in my room those three days,
that's all../..Of course, I'll have to stay in my room.
Think I'll have any of these fly-by-night maids
waiting on me? I wouldn't trust one of them to
get my medicine for me. But that's all right.
You go ahead. I don't matter any more../..Only
for three days? Does it occur to you, Sarah, that
anything might happen to me during those three
days? But that's all right, you go ahead... You
know I have only you to help me but you can't
expect your children to be grateful../..Who'd she
say was going to be there? George Van Schuyler?
Did you say George Van Schuyler? That is very
funny ... George Van Schuyler once asked you to
marry him, didn't he?../..Then he married some-
body else and they got a divorce. Hoping he'll

ONE WOMAN SHOW   Page 21

ask you again, Sarah? Let me see -- that was 19
years ago, wasn't it? Well, Sarah, you were quite
good-looking then -- you'd be mighty foolish to let
him see you now../..Oh, yes, he'll have changed too.
But then he went to New York to live. His wife
was a Washington Society woman. He led a different
kind of life from yours. I suppose you're wishing
now you'd married him. You seem to forget,
Sarah, that at that time your father had just died
and your brother'd gone to live in California. The
mere question of who was to take care of me may
not seem to have occurred to you. You're 43 years
old, Sarah, and you look it. Well, I think I'll get on
down to the church ... Oh, look, look, who's coming.
It's that new woman -- she's coming back from golf.
I'm going to speak to her... Ahem! Good morning.
Nice day, isn't it? I haven't had the pleasure of
meeting you but I've been coming to this hotel for
so many years, I always speak to the new arrivals.
I believe you've got the room across the hall from
me. There used to be mice in that room. Hope
they got rid of them. You staying for long?../..
Well, I expect you'll find it rather quiet. Oh, I'm
Mrs. Brown and this is my daughter Sarah and
you're.../...Mrs. Van Schuyler? Well, we'll be seeing
you again, Mrs. Van Schuyler. Well, Sarah..
You know who that is now! Still think you'll go

Page 22   ONE WOMAN SHOW

visit Mary Pinkney and renew your acquaintance with George Van Schuyler. ... Well, I think I'll be going down to the church now! There's one thing I do pride myself on -- I never miss a Saturday arranging the flowers on the altar!

- - - - - - - -

BEING PRESENTED

This monologue was created when the "Presentation Courts" were still being held in Buckingham Palace. At these ceremonies certain select British "debutantes" (most of them young, but a few not at all young) were presented to the King and Queen, later the Queen and the Duke of Edinburgh. They were obliged to wear the traditional formal attire, a gown with a long train, long white gloves and on their heads the "Three Feathers" of the Prince of Wales. Ladies of other nationalities, through their embassies, occasionally wangled an invitation and could thenceforth boast of being "Presented." This is an impression of an American woman who has been thus fortunate. She is middle-aged, hails from Nebraska, talks with a hearty Middle-Western accent and has a delicious sense of humor about herself. The props, carried on by the performer, consist of a pair of long white gloves, three white ostrich feathers attached to a comb and a flowing white veil. To this I added a white feather fan.

ONE WOMAN SHOW

Introduction

> BEING PRESENTED takes place in a
> London Hotel bedroom. A middle-aged
> American woman in formal attire is
> standing before a mirror fussing with
> three white ostrich plumes and a veil
> in preparation for being presented to
> the Queen and the Duke of Edinburgh.

NOW BLANCHE, BE HONEST. Would you wear these this way or this way?./.this way?./.this way? (KNOCK) Oh, that's the waiter. Come in. Want anything, Blanche? Sure? Well, I do. Waiter, I want a whiskey and soda, a double whiskey and soda .... and hurry, will you? Now then, which way did you say you liked these, Blanche? This way? I wish you could wear 'em drooping ... or spread out, kinda ...But you can't ... you gotta wear 'em this way. Ha! Wait'll Vergil sees me, he'll die!../..Oh my dear, he thinks this all nonsense. You know Vergil. Last week I tried to drag him to Ascot .. would he go? He spent the entire afternoon reading old Chicago Tribunes in the American Club. (STRAP.) Oh glory! ... that was my shoulder strap../..oh could you, Blanche? It's just where I can't reach it. Oh no,

ONE WOMAN SHOW   Page 25

my dear, Vergil thinks I'm crazy to be doing this ...
I shouldn't wonder if he was right. But then,
Blanche ... you know, Uncle Joe being a Senator
and knowing the Ambassador ... I thought it'd be
an experience ... Holy mackerel! I guess it will be.
Can't you find the strap, Blanche? It's this damn
bra that woman talked me into buying in Paris.
D'you want a pin../..or d'you want a needle and
thread? Well wait! Here's a needle and thread.
Might as well get sewn in for the winter. Oh no,
my dear, all these lovely old traditions are utterly
lost on Vergil. He'd choose a Big League game any
day instead. He's the kind that'ud rather have a
Coca Cola than all the "fine champagne" in the
world. Oh thank you, Blanche. Now how do I
look?../..I strongly suspect you of lying, Blanche,
but I'll take your word for it ... I don't mind telling you I'm getting a little../..Well, no, but I've
had happier moments..//..my train? No, it's meant
to be like that. It's all part of the uniform. Ha!
Kinda funny, isn't it? Hope I don't trip over it.
(GASP OF HORROR.) Say, wouldn't it be awful
if I tripped? Oh Lord, I wish they'd hurry with
that whiskey and soda. I tell you I need it ... that
long wait in the Mall out there. I wish Mrs.
Shuster and I could take a flask with us../..Oh no,
it's one of those things that isn't being done, I

Page 26 ONE WOMAN SHOW

guess. If the British can stand it, I can. What's
the use of being born in Nebraska if you haven't
got guts! (GARTER GOES.) That back garter's
come unfastened again. Blanche, could you? ...
Thanks lots../..I can't reach it. With this girdle on
I might as well be wearing armor from the Tower.
Oh my gloves! (PICKS THEM UP.) ... (PULLS ON
LEAVING THE HANDS DANGLING.) Yes, they're
a part of it, God help me ... I haven't worn gloves
like these since the Metropolitan Opera Company
came to Omaha! Can't you find the garter? ...
Well, just keep angling for it ... you'll find it.
Listen! Here comes Vergil ... Uhuh. I know his
walk. I was hoping he wouldn't come 'til after I'd
left. No such luck. (ENTER VERGIL.) Hello,
Verge. Didn't I tell you, Blanche? There's no
circus parade at all, Vergil, you know perfectly
well where I'm going. I'm going to Buckingham
Palace. I'm going to be presented to the Queen.
.../...Hear him, Blanche? He says "What a present
that'll be!"../..Yeah, Blanche is here. Back of me.
She's conferring on me the Order of the Garter../...
What are you laughing at, Verge? I don't see what's
so damn funny about me. Just because you're so
provincial ... Well ... there. (TO BLANCHE.) Now.
How do I look? (TURNS ON VERGIL.) ../..What
do you mean I look like hell?../..How do *I* think I

ONE WOMAN SHOW			Page 27

look? I think I look kinda cute.../...These? These
are the three feathers of the Prince of Wales../..Lend
them to me? Of course he didn't lend them to me.
They're part of the Court costume. Don't you like
them?../..Verge! What a fool you are! They don't
make me look like a circus pony at all! Now
Vergil, don't get me upset! It's all right for you
and Blanche. You don't have to go through with
this thing. But I do, and I don't mind telling you
I'm three jumps ahead of a fit!../..Why am I doing
it? Because I owe it to my home town. The near-
est anyone from there'll ever get to royalty again
is seeing them on television. Jerusalem! The
things I've done for Nebraska! (KNOCK.) Come
in! Thank you, waiter. Just put it here, will you?
That's all, thanks.../...That is a double whiskey and
soda ... And it's for me ... all of it. I might as well
be drunk as the way I feel. (POURING IT OUT.)
Any minute now, I'm sharing a car with another
American woman. She's a Mrs. Shuster ...
Milwaukee. Beer! My dear, barrels of it! She's
coming by for me ... and we're going to play gin
rummy on the way. You know, you have to wait
for ages and ages ... In the Mall ... in your car../..
No, Vergil, we're not going in a hearse and you're
not funny!../..Well, you drive to the Palace ... and
you all wait in a big room--at least that's what they

tell me--then you all file past the Queen and the
Duke of Edinburgh.../...You don't say anything to
them. They merely bow and you curtsey. Mrs.
Shuster and I've been taking lessons in it. You
ought to see us. Well, we're about evenly matched.
She weighs more, but I creak more. Oh! My knees!
I forgot all about them. ... They crack. (DEEP
KNEE BEND.) It's that old arthritis, you know. If
I do this often enough they won't crack when I
curtsey.../...You don't want the Queen to hear my
knees crackling, do you? It's not the kind of notice
I want, thank you. (WALK ABOUT.) Lord, I wish
this were all over. I've got real stage-fright about
this curtseying business. You know, Vergil, that
left knee of mine. Well, you've seen yourself what
it does sometimes...I can get down all right.
Question is can I get up? What'll happen if I can't?
Will they just leave me there? Say, listen Blanche,
will you go with me to the photographers tomorrow?
I'm having my photograph taken in all this.../...
Well, I thought they might want it for the Sunday
paper at home.../...No, Verge, not the funny sheet!
Why? Don't you think it'll be nice to have my
picture in Court Costume?.../...For the children...
it'll amuse them../...I don't know what you mean
"And how." (BELL.) There's the phone. I bet
it's Mrs. Shuster. Hello? Yes...What? All right.

Tell her I'll be right down. Yes. It is my car. I wish it were an ambulance. Vergil, help me with my wrap. You two are going to the Music Halls, aren't you? Well, whatever you see at the Alhambra'll be nothing to the act I pull at Buckingham. Let's see...I've got my gloves and my fan... Try my knees once more. Oh Lord! That started a run in my stocking. No, I haven't time to change now, I'll fix it with spit in the car! Well, good-bye, you two. I tell you I feel like one of the Light Brigade..."Theirs not to reason why, theirs but to do or die"... Into the jaws of death, into the mouth of hell, strode the Nebraskan!

HOMEWORK

> *This sketch is self-explanatory representing a mother sitting by a table mending or reading and struggling to help her little boy with his homework. It needs no regional accent and no hand props unless the performer prefers a book and pencil and paper on the table to use with the school arithmetic problem.*

Introduction

Homework. It might occur any evening in any American household.

YES DEAR? ... WHAT IS IT DARLING?.../...I can't understand you, Junior, you shouldn't mumble your words so.../...Oh, mother's too tired to come upstairs, dearie, you'll have to come down. Hello, son../..What, dear../..What is it, darling? Ummmmm? What is it you want, Junior?.../... An arithmetic problem? Well, just put your mind on it.../...Junior, darling, never say can't!. But I'm sure it can't be as hard as all that... Well, all right.../...Come, sit on the arm of my chair. Mother just loves to help her little boy! Which is it, number 9? . . . Let's see now, Junior . . . Turn that way a minute . . . I wish you could see behind

ONE WOMAN SHOW Page 31

your ears.../...I never saw anything so disgraceful
in all my life!.../...This morning. Well, you'll have
to wash them again at night. I can't imagine what
you do to them during the day. Do you play
games, dear, in which you put your ears to the
ground?.../...Now, Junior, please try to remember.
Which is it, number 9?. Let's see now . . .
(MUMBLING.) "Three boys a, b and c were...
when one...A...twice as many as B...B...that if C...
three of his marbles...A...then...that if C...seven...
the...number...would be twice as many as C then
had left...How many marbles did each boy have?"
Well, darling that's very simple! That's rather a
neat little problem. You see all you have to do
is...Yes, all you have to do...All right. Now we'll
read this through carefully, and you listen. "Three
boys, A, B and C were playing"...Don't kick the
chair like that...you're not listening.../...No, because you can't listen and kick at the same time.
"Three boys, A, B and C were playing at marbles"
...They were playing at marbles... "When A remarked that if B gave him one of his marbles B
would have twice as many as A then had..."
Well, that was nice... "B then remarked that if
C gave him three of his marbles, B would have
twice as many as C had...A then remarked that if
C gave him 7 of his marbles, the number that A

would have would be twice as many as C would have left. How many marbles did each boy have?" ... Well, darling... What you do is, you *add.* I mean *multiply...* I don't know...maybe we'd better divide. "Three boys A, B and C were playing at marbles when A remarked that if B" ... Why do they always have to be called A, B and C? The trouble with these problems is they don't make them interesting enough... They ought to give them names.../... All right, Junior, *we'll* give them names -- we'll call them -- Let's see, now, A, B and C. We'll call them Andrew, Boris and Conrad.../...Boris? It's a perfectly good name, Junior. It's Russian.../...No, it isn't necessarily the name of a police dog.../...Bill? All right, then, Bill. All right, then... Andrew, Bill and Conrad..."Now Andrew remarked that if Bill"... Junior! Don't do that! Can't you remember to use your handkerchief?.../...You did that the other day when Mrs. Darlington was here and I was never more mortified in all my life... I'm sure the little Darlington boy doesn't do that.../...Well, never mind about the little Darlington boy...go get mother's button basket over there...The button basket, dear...Oh, Junior, if it were a snake it would bite you. The button basket. That's it. Don't spill the buttons. And you sit over there. Now these buttons are marbles.../...Because I say so!

I'm Andrew. Here, give me your hands. You're
Bill, and here's Conrad over here. Now you give
me one marble.../...Any will do, Junior! Now you
have twice as many as I have.../...I don't *know* how
many marbles there are...there are X marbles. X is
the marbles.../...Junior, please don't argue with me...
I remember perfectly we spent years and years in
school letting X equal something../..Well, it's an
expression. "Let X." Like "Let Go."../...I can't
help it if Miss Meebles has you do it a different
way, mine is the old-fashioned way and I know I'm
right...Now, then, Conrad gives you three marbles.../...
You've given all yours to Conrad?....What did you
give them to Conrad for? He gives you three and
you give me one...I'm Andrew...Did you dance
with the little Andrews girl in dancing school today?
../..Oh now, son, I told you particularly...You don't
hate her at all...that's a very ungentlemanly thing
to say.../...Her nose doesn't stick up...When she's
eighteen you'll call it retrousee and think it's
beautiful...Did you take three from Conrad?.../...
Well, take three from Conrad. Now, Conrad gives
me seven...one...two, three...oh,pick up that one
that fell...Oh, that's one I've been hunting for weeks
to put on your father's coat...put that over here...
Now, Conrad has given me seven...he's given you
three...Junior...do you have to make that noise?...

Page 34   ONE WOMAN SHOW

That queer bubbling noise? Well, it's very unattractive...And Junior, if you don't stop kicking this table I shall do this wrong purposely to punish you...No, *please pay attention!* (SHE IS GETTING MORE AND MORE DESPERATE.) Andrew then remarked that if Conrad gave him seven of his marbles the number that Andrew would have would lack three of being twice as many as Conrad would have left -- of all the fool things for a boy to remark when he's playing marbles! He couldn't have been healthy. It's not normal for a boy to talk like that -- "Lack three of being twice as many... twice as many..." Junior, I don't see why you don't try to use a little more gumption and work this out for yourself...I'm just worried sick about your laziness. They tell me that you take no interest in your work. Here you come to me with a perfectly simple little arithmetic problem../..Of course I can do it but I think you ought to! Oh wait a minute -- wait a minute! I think I *can* do it! Now let me see. You gave me one and he gave me three...don't interrupt me (MUMBLING.) "equals five plus four...lack..subtract...and...equals ZERO!" There's the answer to the problem...the answer is ZERO../..the question? Well, dearie, the question was..."How many marbles did each boy have?" Oh Junior! You tell Miss Meebles

ONE WOMAN SHOW

that that's a perfectly stupid arithmetic problem..
and one that would fit you in no way for future
life. Now, you've got to go upstairs to bed. I'll
do it and bring it up to you. You go on up to bed.
...I'll be up...I'll be up when I've got a better answer.
(PICKING UP TELEPHONE AND DIALING A
NUMBER.)...Hello. Is this the Racquet Club? Is
Mr. Marshall there?.../...This is Mrs. Marshall.../...
He's in the card room?../..Well, next time he's
dummy will you ask him to../..he's right there?
Well, let me speak to him, will you please?...Hello,
George? Hello, darling. Have you got a minute?
Well, have you got a pencil?../..Junior just came to
me with an arithmetic problem and I can't do it...
Now I'll read it to you../..Oh don't be a lemon,
George, yes you can, while the others are playing
this hand. It won't take you a minute. It's
terrible!..."Three boys A, B and C were playing
at marbles../..Marbles, George../..Now, don't be
funny! When A remarked that if B gave him one
of his marbles B would have twice as many as A
then had../..Yes. B remarked that if C gave him
three of his marbles, C would have twice as many
as B had../..Now wait'll you hear what A said! A
then remarked that if C gave him 7 of his marbles
the number that A would have would be twice as
many as C would have left....How many marbles

did each boy have?... /..No, dear. He gave him
one../..Who gave who what?../..Oh, yes, I see../..
I see.. /..yes../.. Yes../..And C had 19?../..Oh, that's
too divine! Having a good time, dear?../..That's
right../..Yes, I'll leave the key under the door../..
Goodnight...Oh George, how many did A have?../..
I see. That's too divine. (SMILES BRILLIANTLY.)
Goodnight, dear...Now, Junior, Mother's worked
this all out for you!

A LADY EXPLORER

This sketch was written during the early thirties. A well-known English lady novelist had gone on a much publicized safari into darkest Africa with her husband and a group of explorers. Elated over her experiences, she came to the U.S. on an illustrated lecture tour. This sketch is an impression of one of her lectures illustrated with slides. She is a genial lady, speaks with a "veddy-veddy" British accent, is quite vague and prone to emitting an occasional idiotic laugh. For details of presentation, costume and hand-props see Appendix, p. 124.

Introduction

This sketch, A LADY EXPLORER, is an impression of an English lady novelist who went on an African safari and was subsequently booked on an illustrated lecture tour to share her experiences with the American public.

OH, IS IT TIME FOR ME? Oh, I'm so sorry! Ahem! Ladies and gentlemen, it gives me great pleasure to be in this magnificent country of yours.

ONE WOMAN SHOW

...Ha! I may as well tell you at the start ... I've never lectured before. When I mentioned going on a lecture tour to my husband and Sir Harry with whom I made this little dash through Bogandia ... they said to me, "Billy" ... Ha! They always call me Billy ... rather sweet of them ... they said Billy, the one place for you to lecture is America .. they're so very, very tolerant of lectures in America. So you see if it weren't for this magnificent country of yours I shouldn't be here at all../...Well, as dear Mr. Gladstone said, "Let's get down to cases." ... Ha! I think dear Mr. Gladstone said that. I'm sure you're all most anxious to know just where Bogandia is and I shan't keep you waiting any longer. You know, I clean forgot a map! Ha! I'm frightfully sorry! So I shall have to ask you to imagine your map of Africa ...are you imagining it? ... Well, here you'll notice is Madagascar and here is Cape Town...dear old Cape Town...Oh, you're getting this all backward, aren't you?...Here is Madagascar and here...You know, I simply can't do it that way, I shall have to turn my back and show you this way. (TURNING BACK AND MAKING VAGUE GESTURES.) Here is Madagascar and here is Cape Town...Now up in there is the Rand...No, I beg your pardon, the Rand's more up in there...and just about in here is Bogandia...Is that quite clear?...Bogandia is a province of...er...

ONE WOMAN SHOW   Page 39

well, it doesn't belong to England...er, .. Ha! I really
don't know who it belongs to...but at any rate there
it is.... (CLICKER)...The Bogandians are all black...
Beautifully black. Their main interest is headhunting
and with it all they're rather dears. (CLICKER) Er,
I think we're quite ready for the first picture. You
know this is rather a lark...I have no idea what the
first picture's going to be! (PAUSE AND ANOTHER
CLICK.) Ha, Mr. Mechanician! We're quite ready!...
Oh yes, I *do* know what that is! That's my husband.
(CLICK) Setting out in his Mazoo from Cape Town.
(CLICK) Ah, next picture...do you?...Yes. Oh yes.
This is where our first tragedy occurred...fording the
Magaroomy River. Sir Harry tripped on a wet stone
...poor darling, his shoes were rather too large for
him! His pack was open and before we knew it the
quinine had fallen into the Magaroomy River and
dissolved...(CLICK) Er, Mr. Mechanician, would
you like me to clap my hands so?...Well, I'm afraid
you'll have to be a little more sharp. Oh, this is
our cook and our water-carrier...Yenbo and his
cousin Chenbo...or was it Kenbo? ... No! It was
Chenbo...You know they hate to have their photo-
graphs taken, so I slipped up on them and took this
picture and they never knew it...it was naughty of
me! Yenbo is the one with his mouth open! Oh -
Chenbo has his mouth open too! These people are

Page 40   ONE WOMAN SHOW

sort of left-hand cousins of the Gru-Gru tribes of
the Belgian Congo...They have those quaint Swahili
customs, the yearly fermenting of the breadfruit..the
throwing of old women to the crocodiles..after all,
one can't blame them for that...and all that sort of
thing. (CLICK AGAIN.) Er, mechanician...would
you like me to wave my hankie...because I really
think...Oh! This is our first head-hunter! We were
trekking along through a thicket of Guantamottle
bushes when we came upon him just outside of
Gampo-Gampo...As you know, Gampo-Gampo is
the capital of Bogandia...Bogandia is shaped rather
like this and up here is Gampo-Gampo. He greeted
us in that charming native manner of theirs saying
"Lahala gwampa lo"...Ha! I don't know how many
of us speak Swahili...meaning "Greetings...how do
you do?" And we replied "Lahala gwampa lee"
meaning "Same to you, old chap." You'll notice
he's wearing only a little loin thing of Kawagoochee
leaves. I hope you don't mind! They tell me I have
to be most frightfully careful about that sort of
thing in America...I think maybe we'd better have
the next picture, please! Oh these are the Choombi-
Kang...or devil dancers...you needn't be afraid..They
aren't real devils! Ha! You'll notice they're dancing
the Campo-Zong-Zong. The young men stand on the
right and the young women on the left....No! I beg

ONE WOMAN SHOW   Page 41

your pardon! It's the young women who stand on the left and the young men on the right...Ha! That's just what I said, isn't it? It's the young men who stand on the left and the young women on the right ...of course, according to where you're standing and watching them. Then the young men take three rather short little running steps...oh, it's a fascinating dance! And then the old men...the old men bring up breadfruit shells filled with steaming choompi...Have you ever tasted choompi? It tastes rather like hot vodka...it's very...er...intoxicating...They, er, they gave us quite a bit of it...and...oh yes, the dance... well, I don't seem to remember very much more about the dance...I think perhaps we'd better have the next picture...Oh, this is Sir Harry dressed in his Oomlah. (CLICK.) This is your speaker's husband dressed in his Oomlah...rather smart these Oomlahs, don't you think? They're made of old banana-peelings...frightfully old banana peelings...er...braided together with some native something or other. (CLICK SEVERAL TIMES.) (START GETTING TANGLED UP WITH BEADS ABOUT HERE - CONTINUE ON TO END.) Mr. Mechanician... suppose you don't wait for me...just send them right along...one right after the other...I think that would be best because otherwise we can't...Oh, this is the the native king and his concubi! ... and his wives ...

Page 42   ONE WOMAN SHOW

This! ... er, I didn't see which that one was...I say, he is sending them right along, isn't he? That was out on the Veldt...That was a giraffe...er...that last was upside down...Oh dear, he's going so fast...I... er...Oh! Whatever's happened? Is the young man ill? ../... The fuse?.../...But we can't have it blowing out...Can't you use it a little longer and blow it out later on? ../... I'm frightfully sorry... I'm afraid we shall have to call this an intermission... I didn't know. If you don't mind I think I shall just take the time to glance over my notes..you know I didn't look at them before I came, so I wasn't quite...well, cheerio ...I shall see you (TRAIL OFF.)

- - - - - - - - - -

MONTE CARLO

This is a characterization of an old woman who has been living on a pension in Monte Carlo for years. She is hooked on gambling and each night finds her in the Casino playing the roulette wheel until her money runs out and even then she haunts the place along with other sad derelicts. When her monthly allowance arrives, she goes back to spend it all on the wheel confident she'll eventually break the bank. She should be played with an old crone's cracked voice and the sort of English accent ex-patriots acquire after years on the Continent. When playing this, I used to rumple up my hair (in view of the audience) put on a floppy battered hat, a tatty beaded dog collar around my neck and over my shoulders a weather-beaten feather boa.

Introduction

This is an impression of one of the old gambling women one occasionally finds in the Casino at Monte Carlo. The old woman speaks :

CROUPIER! CROUPIER! A CHEVAL! Sur le huit et neuf et dix louis sur le noir. That's right -- that's right. Wonder why they're playing the 20

Page 44   ONE WOMAN SHOW

so heavily. Ach! Can't be the 20 -- it's bound to be the 8 or 9 unless I've counted wrong again - Let's see in my book ... 8 came up here once and it came.... (THE WHEEL TURNS. SHE WATCHES INTENTLY.) Aha! Aha! Qu'est ce que c'est? The 30 black? Well, I get my ten louis back but I lose on the 8 and 9. I must mark that 30 in my system book ... that makes 5 times in the last ...What have I dropped? ... Oh merci, Monsieur...merci...je ne sais pas pourquois mais ce soir .../... Oh you speak English? I was merely saying I don't know why but I seem to be losing everything tonight including my bets, I'm afraid. Thank you very much, young sir. Now shall I risk the 5 or make it across? I think across ... 100 francs on the 4, 5 and 6 across ... Le quatre, cinq, six traversale, croupier! Croupier! He refuses to pay the slightest attention to me, that croupier! I'm trying to put it on the 4, 5 and 6 across.../...If you would? It's rather a stretch and I can't manage the rake any more, I'm afraid. Thank you very much, young sir. He's a wicked man, that croupier. Oh he's a horrid, wicked man! He's one of them that are against me ... lots of them are against me here, you know. They're afraid of this book.../...my system. I'm working out an amazing system here, you know. You've had a run of luck ...I've noticed you... /...Was it you who won so much last week?

ONE WOMAN SHOW   Page 45

Oh, you've only just arrived? ... Oho, I thought I hadn't
seen you before. Oh good heavens! I must play! It's
time for me to play.../...That's right, I have played? I
forget sometimes, you know. (WATCHING THE
WHEEL.) Is it the 5? It's bound to be the 5 according to my figures ... is it the 5 ...Did he say 19? Of
course it's 19../...I forgot it was this croupier../.. Oh
that was stupid of me, I should have played the 19!
Why you must have won 5 mille.../...you bad boy!
You've got a system! And you look so young to have
a system! Go on! Tell me how you do it.../...Oh.
You never played before? Then, that's it! The wheel's
good to beginners. That's how it catches you. Mustn't
let the wheel catch you unless you can work out a
system like mine and that takes years! Years!.../...
Try a carre this time..../... Le vingt vingt../..et un,
trois et quatre! You've got to sneak up on your luck
.../...Not let it know you're coming. It's a huzzy, the
luck! One year it came for me every time the Mistral
blew. Oh you may smile, but I assure you people
talked about it. The Mistral's the wind from the
Rhone Valley.../...makes everybody cross and hate-
ful. But it blew the wheel right for me. People
talked about it. You *are* plunging! Are you an
American? You Americans always plunge.../...I
knew one who plunged over the Upper Corniche
road! Ha-ha! (WHEEL.) Now look! Mark my words.

Page 46   ONE WOMAN SHOW

It will be the 21../..the 21../..the 21../..the../..the 10!
However could that be? I could have staked my life
on its being the 21! (CONSULTING SYSTEM NOTE-
BOOK.) 21 comes up here once and it came up here
.../...Oh! Ach! Oh! I can't see anything but a perfect
mess of numbers! Steady! Steady! I shall have to
stop and take an aspirin. There, that's better! Plenty
of time to take an aspirin later../..Sleep better if I
take it later../..there! Oh well, that was only 100
francs../..good heavens, young man, you've won again
.../...Thousands! Thousands! That's almost a pity.
You're a nice lad. Have you got a girl in America?
I'll wager. I've got a lad.../...In England. Only he's
a middle-aged lad and he's got a wife.../...Brrr! She's
a bad thing. She tells him I'm a cross old witch and
he believes her. Someday they'll see. Someday when
I've worked out my system! I'll try a column this
time, too tired to figure any more. Premiere Colonne!
Look 'ere! Why don't you stop. You've won a lot../..
Too much fun, eh? Where's that nice boy, Young
Beauseant.../...You ought to meet him.../...He always
stops and says good evening. I wonder.../...*What* am
I talking about! He can't! He shot himself 2 days
ago, silly boy. Oh they do, my dear. The stories you
hear aren't fairy-tales. I've been coming here for
years.../...I'd live here only I've got to get away from
the numbers. I start seeing them after I go to bed at

ONE WOMAN SHOW   Page 47

night. Thousands of numbers dancing! Dancing!
They're almost pretty. But I don't get very far, I
always come back. (WHEEL.) Now mark my words!
It'll be one of the numbers in the first column../..
That's how I get my money back at the end of the
evening. Aha! The 25! Centre Column. Well, that'll
do me for tonight. What you going to do with all
your money, young man, buy something for your
girl, eh? Watch out you don't lose it. You'll stop
when you start losing?.../...Aye, they all say that.
Wait a bit! Before you play again, my dear, I'm going
to ask you a favor. I'm going to ask if you'll take me
out for a breath of air../..Yes, now. Pity to take you
away while you're winning but I'm rather an old
thing and I can't walk very well alone../..Thank you,
my dear. My head's spinning and I want to take an
aspirin to steady it.../...they won't let you take a
pill in the Casino, you know.../...Oh good heavens,
no!.../...They think you're swallowing poison and
send you to the police station to have it pumped out.
This way, sir. This way's past the Comptoire.../...
Hadn't you better cash in your winnings on the
way out?.../...Oh I wouldn't come back if I were
you. After all, you've had your fun. I thought you
might have an ice with me at the cafe outside. You
get a fine breeze from the sea. I want to hear about
that girl in America.../...And I'm going to tell you

about my system. I'm working out an amazing system. I'm going to break the bank someday like the man in the song. I expect you're too young to remember that song. This way! This way!

- - - - - - - - - - -

THE FACTS OF LIFE

This is an attempt to portray what the mother of an eight or nine year old boy goes through when she attempts to tell him the "facts of life." She is played naturally without any particular characterization or accent. There are no hand props. The cocktail shaker and glass and the telephone are merely indicated by gesture.

Introduction

This characterization is called THE FACTS OF LIFE. It takes place in a suburban household anywhere.

(SPEAKER ENTERS FLUTTERING, MOVES ABOUT NERVOUSLY A BIT. PICKS UP PHONE AND PUTS IT DOWN.) OH DEAR! (MORE UNCERTAIN MOVEMENT.) EMMA! OH EMMA! HAS ORRIN COME HOME FROM SCHOOL YET! .../... When he comes send him in here, will you? I want to see him just as soon as he gets back so be sure he doesn't run out to play before he's talked with me.../...All right, Emma. (EMMA STARTS OUT.) Oh Emma...er.../...I wonder if you'd.... would you mix up a cocktail?...Uhuh a cocktail.

-49-

ONE WOMAN SHOW

I'm not feeling very ... I just thought I'd like a cocktail....I tell you....You just bring the shaker and things and I'll mix it.../...No, just for me. And you might bring a bottle of Coca-Cola for Orrin...Ha! Sounds like quite a party, doesn't it?...Thank you, Emma. (EMMA EXITS. STILL UNCERTAIN.... A FEW "Oh, dear.") (SPEAKER PICKS UP PHONE AND DIALS.) Hello, Maisie, is this you?....Is it? Well, this is me.../...Fine. How are you? That's fine. How's Johnnie?.../...Oh Orrin is fine - we all are.... er...well I don't know that I *am* fine. I'm awfully nervous.../...No, I'm not sick or anything, I'm just, you know, upset.../...Well, nothing's happened yet... but something's going to happen...What's that?.../... Am I going to have a....Oh good heavens no! At least I hope not! No, it's....it's something I have to do. That is, it's something Miss Sproul says I have to do.../...Miss Sproul.../...Orrin's teacher, and, Maisie, she's awfully progressive. It seems they believe that all parents ought to....well, she wants me to tell Orrin all about.....Maisie, have you got any books? .../... Oh I don't mean books, I mean...well, books. You know the kind they don't sell in stores...you have to send for them and they come in a plain wrapper...you hope.../...all about life. Miss Sproul says Orrin's old enough to be told about life and honestly, Maisie, I don't know what to tell him../..

Well I'm glad you think it's so funny.../...Why, Maisie,
Mother never told me anything! You know what she
and Dad are like../..I don't think they even knew about
such things. Of course I don't exactly know how they
accounted for me but...(EMMA APPEARS WITH THE
COCKTAIL THINGS.) Wait a minute, Maisie. Thank
you, Emma. Just set those down on the table over
there, will you please, Emma? What, Emma? No,
I'll mix it. That's all, thank you, Emma. Sorry, Maisie,
I was talking to Emma... Well, Maisie, have you been
through all this with Johnny?.../...You have? Oh
aren't you modern! What did you tell him? How
did you go about it?../..Bees? What do you mean,
bees? Oh I'd forgotten about bees. Of course. Well
do bees do it?.../...I mean did bees give Johnny the
idea?../..I guess bees are the solution then.../...Bees
or puppies. Thanks for the tip. I'm bracing myself
with a cocktail. Want to come over later?.../...All
right. Bye, dear. (CROSS TO SHAKER AND
START MIXING COCKTAILS. ORRIN IS SEEN
OUTSIDE.) Orrin! Orrin! Come here, dear. Didn't
Emma tell you I wanted to see you?.../...Then where
are you going?../..No, you're not going next door to
Johnny's...you're coming right in here with me../..
Because I say so. Orrin! (CLAPPING HANDS.)
Come back here.../...(FURIOUS.).../...Orrin, you
come back here this minute! (ORRIN RETURNS.)

Page 52   ONE WOMAN SHOW

Now, then. (CHANGE FROM RAGE INTO SICKLY
SWEETNESS.)../..Come in, dear. Now you and
Mother are going to have a lovely little talk.../...
(ANGER AGAIN.) You're not going next door to
Johnny's; you're going to sit right down in that
chair!.../...I don't care if Johnny has **ten** new Beebee
guns.../...***This is more important than beebee guns!***
(AGAIN CHANGE INTO HONEY.) And it's a lot
more interesting.../...How do you know? You don't
even know what it is. (CONTINUING WITH SHAKER,
etc.) Sit down, honeybunch and make yourself
comfortable. (ORRIN HESITATES.) SIT DOWN!!
And please don't pout. You know I hate pouting!
Now. Mother has a nice bottle of Coca-Cola for you
here. Don't you want a nice bottle of Coca Cola?
Oh. I was going to have a cocktail and I just thought
it would be nice if you had some coke with me. Oh,
just having a cocktail.../...Nobody, just you and me.
.../...It isn't queer at all, Orrin. We ought to do this
more often. Well, (POURING HERSELF A GOOD
ONE.) now what I wanted to talk to you about was..
er...something we're going to talk about (FIRST
GULP.)..Now, Orrin....take your feet off that chair..
you've been told a hundred times. There! Now
Orrin, precious (ANOTHER GULP.) This is
nothing to get upset about. (GETTING UPSET
HERSELF.) Nothing at all to get upset about.

ONE WOMAN SHOW   Page 53

Orrin, Mother thinks you should know...(ORRIN LOOKS FRIGHTENED.) Don't look so scared, dear.../...it's nothing you've done../..No, this is something Miss Sproul's asked Mother to talk to you about ../..No, darling, this time it doesn't happen to be your report. And by the way, I'm glad you mentioned that. How any one boy could get so many demerits .../...Well, never mind that now../..I'm not interested in who brought the dead mouse to school; you were the one who put it in Miss Sproul's desk../..But never mind all that, we must stick to the subject. And that's another thing, Orrin, Miss Sproul says you never stick to a subject...here you are talking about dead mice instead of sticking to the subject../..Well, I'm *getting* to the subject if you'd only pay attention. (PAUSE.) Orrin (POURS ANOTHER DRINK.) Orrin, this is about having puppies../..No! No! No! We're *not!* I'm not saying we're going to get a puppy ../..Orrin, we had that out with your father last week. And what if we do get a puppy, you won't take care of it../..No, you won't. You didn't take care of the last one. Who's going to train the thing?../..Yes, you think so and so does Daddy, but it all ends up in my having to get up in the middle of the night and clean up after it../..No, we're not having any puppies *and that settles it!* There! Now you see, Orrin, what Mother means about never sticking to a subject?

ONE WOMAN SHOW

Now you're off on puppies../..Did I? Well, I didn't mean puppies to play with, I mean...where puppies come from../..Well, I know they come from the pet shop, but it's before they get to the pet shop. Orrin dear, just hand Mother that cocktail shaker. (AS SHE POURS.) Sure you don't want that Coca-Cola? Thanks. Sit down, dear../..Now about where puppies come from...Orrin, darling, do you know about bees? ../..Yes, they come from hives. But bees, you know, do lots of things../..Do you know what bees do?.../.. Well, only if you frighten them../..That wasn't a bee, it was a hornet../..Yes, Orrin, it was a hornet because I killed it../..all right then, never mind but it *was* a hornet and I'm talking about bees. Now about bees ....they have the loveliest time with flowers. They get all covered with pollen../.. No, the queen doesn't dust them off, that's just the point. They keep the pollen on.../...Well I don't know why, Orrin, but they like it. Then they go from flower to flower all nice and dusty with pollen (GETS A LITTLE HYSTERICAL.) -- pollen -- and you see? That's just what people do../..Men. They go from flower to flower. Oh dear I don't mean that. I don't mean that at all! This isn't getting anywhere. (OUTBURST TO SELF.) Who the devil ever started this bee and pollen talk anyway?../..No darling, I'm not saying you did...I'm not mad at you! No dear I'm not excited../..I *am*

ONE WOMAN SHOW

getting this over...If you'd just sit still and pay attention! Well, I guess I just have to take the bull by the horns. (SLIGHTLY HYSTERICAL...THE TEARS WELLING UP.) No it's not about bulls or cows either.../...I'm not crying. (ORRIN STARTS TO CRY.) For heaven's sakes don't you cry too, Orrin. Stop it, now, stop it! There's nothing to cry about ../..Nothing at all (WIPING EYES AND BLOWING NOSE.) There, you see? Everything's all right. Here, blow on this. There. That wasn't anything to get all excited about,was it now..../..That wasn't ../..What Miss Sproul wants me to tell you../.. Well, Miss Sproul couldn't tell you very well because.... (PLUNGE.) Miss Sproul's never had a baby! Now you know../.. What we're talking about. You see Mother has had a baby and Mother knows. Yes, I guess Miss Sproul knows too but.../...Just what do you mean, "she's awfully dumb if she doesn't?"../.. Why, Orrin Jones,you mean to say you've known all along?../..Where babies come from?.../...Well, why didn't you ever tell me?../..Of course I know but.... Where did you ever hear such things../..Johnny's a very naughty and nasty little boy and I'm surprised that you'd listen to him.../...Well, of course I wanted you to know but I wanted to tell you. I wanted you to get it straight.../...What was that? What did you say then? Yes you did, you said that Johnny had it straight and I hadn't. Why, Orrin Jones, if I weren't so upset I'd spank you. Oh, it's no use ever discussing anything with you.../...No, it isn't.../...You run on out../....Yes, you might as well go to Johnny's, he's done all the harm he can. Go on. Get out. Mother's very disappointed in her little boy. (DIALING THE PHONE.) Maisie, it's over, he's been told ../...not by me, dear.../...by Johnny. Uhuh -- and I guess Johnny didn't go in for any bees and pollen. According to Orrin he could give *me* a few ideas. You'd better come over and help me finish this shaker of cocktails!

- - - - - - - - - - -

MOTORING IN THE 90's

This sketch is a piece of pure, almost slap-stick farce. It requires physical exertion that should be maintained throughout. As soon as the machine catches and gets going, the performer should jiggle rather violently in the manner of a passenger in an early automobile. She should sway when the vehicle is supposedly rounding corners and every now and then go into a visible bounce to indicate a bump in the road. She should employ only one chair, the one with arms which she can clutch in moments of panic. For this sketch I pulled my hair forward to simulate a pompadour, put on a little period straw hat trimmed with bows and roses, securing it with a long hatpin, and tied a large pink ribbon about my neck.

Introduction

This is a scene in the gay nineties when a girl is taken for her first ride in an automobile. She speaks:

OH, MR. FILKINS, IS THAT YOU? Oh, I'm so excited! I'll be down in a jiffy. Oh, Mr. Filkins!

ONE WOMAN SHOW

Good afternoon, I knew by that awful noise it must be you. I just can't tell you how excited I am. I feel like Columbus setting out to discover America. So that's the horseless carriage! Well! Well! Isn't it.....isn't it.....stately. It looks just like the Vanderbilt coach. It's the first one I ever saw. I'm simply dippy about it. The lace curtains are moving. That's mama. Hoo! Hoo! Open the window! She's awfully timid about things like this. At the World's Fair we couldn't get her *near* the Ferris Wheel. Come on out and see the Benzine Buggy, Mama. You know she's got some idea that they blow up. What's that other name for them...Something Greek.../...Automobile. Oh, Mr. Filkins, you just know everything. Come on down off the porch, darling, he says it won't blow up. Dearest, you've got this all mixed up with one of those gas heaters...hasn't she, Mr. Filkins? Isn't it stylish, Mama? Look at those dear little straps coming down from the roof. And oh, here's a place for a carriage whip in case you break down and have to be pulled by a horse.../...Oh, Mamma, really! You know, Mr. Filkins, she's been so worried, she's had to take headache powders all week. Oh, Mamma, come off your perch...You let me go buggy riding alone with gentlemen, and I can't see that there's any difference....after all, a horse is no chaperone. And with those wheels and

ONE WOMAN SHOW

things he has to tend to, he wouldn't have time...I think maybe I'd better get in. Where do I?.../...At the rear? Oh, look at the dear little door at the rear. Isn't that subtle? My, what a high step. I'm afraid I'll have to ask you not to look while I get in, Mr. Filkins...it's such a high step. (SOTTO VOCE TO MOTHER.) Could you see my ankle? Now do I go right through to the box and sit in the left-hand seat? ../..Aye, aye, sir. What?.../...You wish Mr. Dana Gibson could see me? Oh, Mr. Filkins, aren't you fierce. But aren't you coming up too?.../...You have to crank it? Whatever do you mean?.....Oh, look! It's like a coffee mill...has to be ground first. Now, you must tell me what I mustn't do...because my skirt might catch on something that would start it...and I don't know anything about handling the ribbons of a thing like this. When are you going to get in?.../... As soon as it starts? Do you mean as soon as you wind it, it starts right off?.../...Oh, I'm not going to stay in here if it does that.../...No, I'm scared pink. ../..D'you mean you grind it and then jump in while it's going?.../...But what if you missed your step or fainted or something?.../...Oh, I think I'd better.../... Well, if you're sure you can jump in...because if you don't, I'm going to jump out and you'll have to catch me.../...Oh, Mr. Filkins! Aren't you a great one!../.. Can't you make it do what it's supposed to do?

ONE WOMAN SHOW

Wouldn't you like us to ask one of the maids to help you? Poor Mr. Filkins! He's all out of breath from that mean old crank. (IT SUDDENLY STARTS.) Oh mercy me, it's going to start after all....hurry up, get in, Mr. Filkins. It's moving...thank goodness you got in all right. I was so afraid...Goodbye, Mamma. Good....(JOLTING SUBSIDES.) It stopped. Now isn't that too bad. After all that work, too. Tch, tch, tch, -- Oh fudge! Why don't we just sit here? I felt what it was like. My! Such determination! Mamma, I wish you'd go in out of the sun.../...Well, now you stand there and you get to thinking...it always makes you so nervous when you think. That poor man! Why, cranking a horseless carriage is worse than a whole morning with the Indian Clubs. (THE ENGINE BACKFIRES.) Help! It *is* going to blow up!.../.. What? A backfire? I never heard such a noise in all my life. I know it's made me deaf!.../...You don't think it has? Well, I'm not at all sure it hasn't. What happened to Mamma? She didn't get blown up, did... why she's run back onto the porch. I kind of wish I hadn't come, Mr. Filkins. It's making such queer noises and....(THE MACHINE CATCHES. START JIGGLING.) It's going to start! Oh, get in! Get in, Mr. Filkins. Goodbye, Mamma! Oh, we're off! Goodbye my darling! Isn't this wonderful! I feel as if I were flying! (INTENSIFY JIGGLING.)

ONE WOMAN SHOW   Page 61

Mr. Filkins, you're not going to start right off for that corner, are you? Hadn't we better wait for a while before we go 'round a corner? I just don't think I'll look. ...Are we there yet? Are we...Ah! We got 'round it, didn't we? I thought we were going straight into that corner saloon. Well, that's one disaster we avoided! Well! My goodness! Everybody under the sun's looking out of their windows. How does it feel to be king of the highway, Mr. Filkins? Where are we going to go?...Flushing? But, Mr. Filkins, Flushing's four miles from here and I promised Mamma I'd be back in an hour.../...Well, if you think you can make it. It seems awfully reckless to me. Oh, but I like to be reckless. Look! Seven miles an hour! You know we're regular scorchers. Isn't this interesting? Why, those mean little boys! Why are they shouting, "Get a horse." "Get a horse." We don't want a horse! Get a horse yourselves! And oh! Here come Ned Strutter and Abbey Hoag on a tandem bicycle! Ned's latest mash! And it's high time because Abbey's been sweet on Ned for ages....but that's on the strict Q.T. They're scared to death! They're getting off and going up on the sidewalk. Hello, Ned and Abbey...want to come for a ride? Will you look at Abbey...or rather *don't* look at Abbey! She's wearing one of those new bicycle costumes with bloomers! How can she! Why I never thought anyone but an actress would wear

ONE WOMAN SHOW

such a thing! If she isn't a live one! Mr. Filkins, look what's coming. A whole lot of carriages. Why, it's a funeral! Oh, dear me, I don't think we ought to go past a funeral at this spanking pace! Hadn't we better stop?....Hadn't we better stop, Mr. Filkins?../... What...You can't stop? How perfectly awful! What are we going to do? Look...there's one, two...four carriages and a hearse. Can't you stop? The horses on the hearse are starting to shy...This seems awfully bad form! How terrible! Mercy, they're rearing! I just wish the driver wouldn't use such language. Oh, Mr. Filkins! The hearse has run away! It's going down the street lickety-split! The carriages seem to be getting past all right. I don't think they know about the hearse. It'll be a surprise, won't it! Mr. Filkins, do you actually mean you can't stop this thing? What are we going to do...go to and from Flushing till it wears out? And we're going so fast... Look! That thing says nine miles an hour! I can't breathe with this rush of wind over the dashboard. It's worse than a runaway! We're going faster and faster! How are we going to get around this cor..... Couldn't we call for help? The people might jump on and maybe that might slow it down a little.../... Stopped! So we have! Oh! Ah! Huh! Down went McGinty! What are you going to do?.....Mr. Filkins, where are you going? Mr. Filkins, is there something

ONE WOMAN SHOW

the matter with you? You mustn't crawl under the car like that! Are you trying to hide from me?.../...What? .../...Fix the engine? Well, I think that's an awfully queer way of doing things. I'm going to get out../.. Yes, I am too. The thing might start while you're under there and they'd say I killed you....(GETS OUT.) My fault? Whatever do you mean it's *my* fault?.../...Clutch you? I didn't clutch you, Mr. Filkins. I may have touched you, but I didn't clutch you!.../...Mr. Filkins, are you saying the things I think you're saying? I never heard such language in all my life...I'm going home.../...I can't help it if you are talking to the machine...the machine doesn't hear it but I do! Here comes Sam in his buggy....I'm going home with him...Sam! Sam! Will you take me home? I'm going home with Sam, Mr. Filkins..../...I am so! At least he won't crawl under his horse and say terrible things...I'm going home the way the Lord meant me to ride!....And my advice to you is what those little boys said. "Get a horse, Mr. Filkins, Get a horse!"

- - - - - - - - - -

SAILING TIME

This sketch is short and can come in easily as the finish of a program. The action is indicated in the text. It represents a woman who is sailing for Europe on one of the big liners. She is waving and talking . . . . of necessity, at the top of her lungs, to two friends who have come to see her off and are standing below on the dock. The only hand prop needed is a good-sized white handkerchief which she keeps waving.

Introduction

An impression of what takes place at the sailing hour of one of the big liners from New York when a woman up on deck tries to communicate with friends below on the dock who have come to see her and her husband off. At first she scuttles up and down in an attempt to find a place at the crowded railing.

ADA! ADA! YOO-HOO! (SHE MANAGES TO WEDGE HERSELF IN BETWEEN AN INDIGNANT FELLOW PASSENGER.) Well, I'm sorry, but *I've* got friends down there, too! Ada, here I am! Ada, up on deck. You're waving at the wrong person!

ONE WOMAN SHOW

(SHE KEEPS FLUTTERING A HANDKERCHIEF THROUGHOUT THE SKETCH, AT FIRST VIGOROUSLY, TOWARDS THE END WITH DIMINISHING ENTHUSIASM.) You see me now, don't you?.../... I say you see me now, don't you?.../...I've had the worst time trying to make you see me!.../...(AS THE FRIEND FAILS TO CATCH WHAT SHE IS SAYING, SHE GOES INTO EXAGGERATED PANTOMIME.) No! No! I've had the worst time trying to make you *see* me!.../...Ha-Ha you got it! Where's Horace? (SHE PRONOUNCES THE NAME LIKE "HORSE", SPEAKING AS SHE DOES IN A TERRIBLE MIDWESTERN ACCENT.) Where's Horace?.../...***Where is Horace?***.../...No, he got off! He got off when they banged that thing! No, I saw a steward push him off.../...What?.../...Was he what?...Not very; he thought one steward was Bert and he shook hands with him. But he was all right. He could still walk! Be good. Take care of yourself.../...I say take care of yourself .../...What?.../...What?.../..Will I what?.../...Yes, I'll take care of myself! Oh, Ada, there's Horace. He's trying to come back up the gangplank. Stop him. Yoo—hoo, Horace! Ada thought you were lost!../.. Ada thought.../...Ada thought.../...Well, never mind! Be good! Take care of yourself!.../...What? Where's Bert? He's down getting our places at the table../... He is down getting our places at the table. (AS HER

Page 66 ONE WOMAN SHOW

FRIEND AGAIN FAILS TO CATCH THE WORDS SHE GOES INTO THE PANTOMIME OF SITTING AND EATING.) Bert is down....getting our *places*.... at the table....That's right, you got it! We don't want to sit at the Captain's table. Bert doesn't think he'll be able to dress for dinner every night. Ha-ha! (SHE GLANCES OVER HER SHOULDER AND SPIES BERT.) Bert! Here's Bert now! Bert! Bert, here I am!.../...Well, that's all right, just push in! There's Ada and Horace, Bert. Wave to them...go ahead, Bert, Ada's waving to you.../...Horace thinks he is, only he's so tight he's waving to a tugboat. Bert says take care of yourself, Ada.../...Ada says take care of yourself, Bert. (SOTTO VOCE TO BERT.) I wish they'd go. (THEN BACK TO DOCK.) Don't wait!...Don't wait!...Don't.....wait! Never mind! Be good and take care of yourself! Oh Ada, who do you think's on the boat? (NAMES ANY CURRENTLY POPULAR MUSICIAN . REPEATS NAME TWICE.) Everybody's tipping the chief steward to be put near his table.... Isn't that silly? I think it's better to try to get near his deck chair, don't you? Be good! Take care of yourself! Ada, shall I give your love to the Duke of Edinburgh?....Ha ha! I'll give your love to the Duke of Edinburgh! (TURNS TO BERT.) Isn't that a scream, giving Ada's love to the Duke of Edinburgh? Bert, can't you think of something to make them

ONE WOMAN SHOW   Page 67

go? (BACK TO HER FRIENDS.) Don't wait....don't wait!....Don't wait!!!.../...What, you don't mind? Well we don't mind but you don't need to wait. Be good! Take care of yourself! (SUDDENLY CATCHING SIGHT OF SOMEONE DOWN THE DECK.) Oh Ada! There's (REPEATS NAME OF MUSICIAN.) Down there. That's (REPEATS NAME OF MUSICIAN.) (GOES INTO PANTOMIME OF PLAYING A PIANO AND GRINNING MAWKISHLY.) (REPEATS NAME OF MUSICIAN.) That's (REPEATS NAME OF MUSICIAN.) What, Bert?.../...Bert says it isn't. Bert says it's the ship's barber. Can you beat it? There goes the gangplank.../...I say, there goes the gangplank.../...I said there went the gangplank! We'll be gone in a minute! (ASIDE TO BERT.) Thank goodness! Oh Ada, do you still want me to bring you what you said you wanted me to bring you? Well, are you a forty or a forty-two?.../...Are you a forty or.... (THE FOGHORN LETS OUT A LOUD BLAST.) Wait till the foghorn stops. Ada, is it a forty or a forty-two?.../...Well, never mind. (ONE GATHERS THAT THE SHIP IS SLOWLY MOVING AWAY FROM THE DOCK. SHE CONTINUES TO WAVE. BY NOW USING HER LEFT HAND TO SUPPORT HER EXHAUSTED RIGHT ONE.) Well, never mind! Be good! Take care of yourself! (ASIDE TO BERT.) Doesn't Horace look horrible? (PRONOUNCED

Page 68   ONE WOMAN SHOW

"DOESN'T HORSE LOOK WHORE-BULL?") Goodbye Horace. Ada's just furious at him. Goodbye Ada! Be good! Take care of yourself! (THE SHIP IS NOW WELL UNDERWAY. SHE TURNS IN RELIEF TO BERT.) Oh Bert, I hope I never see those two people as long as I live.

- - - - - - - - - - - - - -

AMERICAN ANCESTOR WORSHIP

This sketch is a spoof on American ancestor-worship and is longer and more elaborate than most of the others. It involves moving furniture as well as carrying on props and placing them before beginning the various impersonations. First the performer plays the present-day descendant; then she harks back to characterize the ancestress of whom she is so proud.

Introduction - The Bostonian Descendant

We have all met the woman who takes personal credit for her ancestors, so it might be interesting to find out just who and what they were. We present here examples from each part of the country, East, West, North and South. We start in that cradle of ancestor-worship, Boston. The Descendant is speaking. She is our hostess, a smiling effusive soul with an exaggerated Bostonian accent.

ABBEY DEAR, PASS MISS TWICHELL THE MUFFINS. Do take a muffin, Miss Twichell. You must be utterly exhausted after your splendid talk.

Page 70   ONE WOMAN SHOW

Abbey, wasn't Miss Twichell's talk too marvelous?...
All those inspiring things she told us! I hope you took
notes, Abbey, so you can tell your teacher and the
girls in your class....and then to have been able to
spirit Miss Twichell away for tea and have her all to
ourselves! Abbey, aren't we lucky? The luckiest
people in the world!.../...Ha! Abbey's just fifteen.
She's not at the demonstrative age. But I just can't
get over all those things you told us in your lecture
about the government...those awful, awful taxes! I
do sometimes wonder what our forebears would have
said about conditions nowadays. I'm sure if there
were taxes then, they were nice taxes...not like these
horrid, horrid ones of ours!.../...You've probably
heard our family were among the first settlers in the
Bay Colony../..Ha! Thank you. We all ought to
follow the example of those fine old patriots who
really had the interests of their country at heart. I
mean we should *do* something, shouldn't we? Well,
do have another cup of tea. Abbey, pass Miss
Twichell's cup.../...I beg your pardon?.../...This
teapot? Well, really, what a delightful coincidence
that you should notice it! Because I'll have you know
that this teapot was made by Paul Revere and was
bought directly from him by my great-great-great
grandmother.../...Ha! Abbey's great-great-great-great
grandmother..../....Yes, it really is a fine piece, and

ONE WOMAN SHOW   Page 71

so delicate...have you noticed the spout? Isn't that a
dear, dear spout? It gives one such pride to know
one's direct ancestress had such perfect taste! I love
to think of that splendid woman patriot in those
perilous times.../...because they were awfully perilous.
Think of her going out of her way to buy this pot,
selecting it for its grace and charm. I often wish
Abbey and I could project ourselves back and eaves-
drop on what must have been a delightful little scene!

- - - - - - - - - - - - -

Introduction - The Eastern Ancestress

> She rises and dons a white mop cap. Now
> she is the pioneer ancestress of whom they
> are so proud -- a grim and rockbound early
> settler.

DID I HEAR YOU SAY ONE POUND FIVE, YOUNG
MAN REVERE? Are you crazy? This pot's worth
just seventeen shillings.../...'tis to me.../...Who in the
name of Beelzebub cares about workmanship? It's
the silver interests me.../...The delicacy of the spout?
You're a ninny to've made it so delicate! If you'd
made it bigger and heavier, there'd've been more
silver in it. With coinage scarce as 'tis, a body's bound

to store up silver when she can. I may want to melt this down some day.../...Saints and sinners! Might think 'twas your baby I was plannin' to melt down! Well, I'll give you eighteen shilling for your precious baby.../...Take it back. 'Tain't worth that much. I'll give you nineteen shillings and not a farthing over. More'n it's worth at that. Agreed?.../...No, I'll not melt it down unless I'm driven to it by this crazy government. I'll use it as 'tis for a time at least.../... what for? What it's meant for, you blockhead, to hold tea. Think I'd give up my tea? People here have taken leave of their senses; all this excitement about tea and taxes and representation! I don't understand a word of it and I don't want to. But I want my tea... and what's more, I know where to get it. There's a Portuguese chandler down by the docks...smart fellow. The night those crazy fools rigged themselves up like Indians and dumped perfectly good tea into Boston Harbor, he salvaged three bales of it before it got wet. No siree, I'm not giving up my tea. Well, I'll go get the money. Racy-looking horse you got there, Mr. Revere. What would a hard-working silversmith be doing with a horse like that? Shouldn't think he'd be much use to you. Nineteen shillings for a teapot! Oh well, I c'n always melt it down.

- - - - - - - - - - -

ONE WOMAN SHOW

Introduction - The Western Descendant, A
California Socialite

> She sits majestically in the armchair with a
> lace shawl about her shoulders -- an aristo-
> crat and very conscious of the fact.

IT'S SATURDAY NEXT, THE FANCY DRESS BALL, CONSUELO? And everyone's to go as a character of old California? How charming...and what a pleasure for me to dress my grand-daughter in my great grandmother's old Spanish finery! I'm sure you'll be the belle of the Ball, my dear! I'm glad you're going because it's the social event of the year. The very best people of Pasadena, Santa Barbara and Pebble Beach will be there. I do hope no one makes the mistake of asking anyone from the motion picture colony. It's all very well to be democratic but there are certain standards we Californians must maintain. (PICKING UP HIGH COMB AND TAKING OFF SHAWL.) Now, Consuelo, here we are...the finishing touches for your costume. My great grandmother's...*your* great, great, *great* grandmother's mantilla and comb. You're an extremely lucky lady. Very few so-called Californians are the genuine article. What I mean is, how many families can claim descent from the first Spanish settlers? We mustn't be over proud, but it is a comfort to realize we have pure Castilian blood in our veins...and as you know, it comes direct from Doña Consuelo Rosario de los Juntos y Perez Jesus Maria y *Smith.* Mr. Smith, Doña Consuelo's husband, was an American --- and --- we have few records of him other than that he seems to have been a seafaring gentleman even if he was not a hidalgo. I do so regret that we have no family portrait of Doña Consuelo dressed in her comb and mantilla. The proud Castilian grande dame of the new world!

- - - - - - - - - -

Introduction - The Western Ancestress, A Spanish Prostitute

> She rises, puts on the Spanish comb, throws the lace shawl over it like a mantilla, turns, straightens chair, sits on it facing the audience and leans back as if looking down from an upper window. She is a young whore, gay, vivacious, with a delicious laugh and a strong Spanish accent.

ONE WOMAN SHOW   Page 75

BUENAS NOCHES, SEÑOR.../...MUY BIEN,
GRACIAS. Sí. Speak English poquecito. I shouldn't
let you talk with me.../...Because I don't know you...
But you stand outside my window so long and you
look so nice! I like Americanos. When you come
California? Today? In big clipper ship? You sailor?
Santos cielos! I shouldn't let you talk with me. Norte
Americano sailors bad! Bad! I know. Spanish señorita no can trust (GESTURE).../...Because I know... *I*...
Come in my house? No! No! Let strange man into
my house? Madre de dios, No!.../ .../... Sh! You wake
my baby!.../...Si, Señor. I got baby in house.../...
Husband? (LAUGH.) No, is no husband in house...
../..No, I don't even know your name.../...What you
say it is? (THE WARM LAUGH.) Smith? Every
sailor Norte Americano say his name is Smith! No,
no! Is not your real name. Sailor come to California..
tell Spanish señorita his name is Smith, make love to
señorita...go away...don't come back...don't write...
How's señorita goin' find Mr. Smith, hein? I had a
friend...same name. On clipper ship too.../...No, not
officer...just nice sailor boy like you. But no good.
Say he love me, love me! Make present comb and
mantilla...Carramba! Go away, no come back, this
Mr. Smith!.../...No! I tell you, I no let you come in
my house.../...You give me present?.../...No, I don't

want mantilla...I want reales...you got reales? Real
silver reales?.../...Let me count. Mmmm, maybe...
for just a little while...(THE RAVISHING SMILE.)
...Here is key. First door top of stairs. Only don't
wake my baby. You want know her name?.../...
Same name as me. Consuelo Rosario de los Juntos
y Perez...Jesus Maria y *Smith*!

- - - - - - - - - - - -

Introduction - The Northern Descendant, A
          Suburbanite

>For our view of northern ancestor wor-
>ship, let us go to Lake Forest, a little
>out of Chicago. The Descendant, a
>fashionable suburbanite, is speaking.
>She is assured and breezy. The desk
>is indicated by a gesture.

WHY, THAT'S RIGHT, MY DEAR. You haven't
been out to see us here in Lake Forest for years!
Not since we redecorated. I bet you didn't even
know we'd gone modern.../...Uh-huh, you're right.
Really modern. Of course I love it...But I don't
have to tell you that George simply hates it...Dear
old George! He's one of those men who thinks he's

ONE WOMAN SHOW

got to scream if he sees any modern art. His idea of a beautiful painting is the Stag at Bay.../...The Picasso? I bought it last month and he hasn't even looked at it. Of course George wouldn't know a Picasso from a hole in the ground! Aren't you cute! Well, I think it's a smart room. All the furniture's new, you see....except this little family desk here and, my dear, I thought the decorator'd have a catfit when I said I was going to keep it. Well, Sweetie, it's just an old farm piece, but George and I are sort of sentimental about it, because George's great grandmother brought it to Illinois in a prairie schooner. She and George's great grandfather were among the first pioneers to settle here. You can imagine how she must have loved this little desk to bring it all the way from Connecticut!...and see that mark there? See that? It's from an Indian arrow! Think of her courage. She was just a bride at the time. Setting out in a wagon train into this wild prairie land!..., ... I couldn't either. You know I have a lot of fun imagining her on that hard trek...This family piece stowed away so lovingly in the back of the covered wagon. She so young and brave...sitting up in the driver's seat alongside of her man, a rifle across her knee, ready for anything, the epitome of the pioneer woman!

- - - - - - - - - -

ONE WOMAN SHOW

Introduction - The Northern Ancestress, A
　　　Frightened Pioneer Bride

> The performer rises, ties on a limp sun-
> bonnet and sits on the end of the table,
> her feet braced on the seat of the straight
> chair. Throughout she should sway and
> go through motions as though on a jolt-
> ing wagon. She is young and timid. She
> speaks:

WHERE ARE WE NOW, GEORGE? No, I don't
want to look at the view. Every view's the same.../...
(SQUIRMING.) My foot's gone to sleep.../...No,
I'll stay back here.../...You know I don't want to
ride up there, George. That woman in the wagon
ahead of us was up with her husband on the driver's
seat...and you know what happened to her...an arrow
right through her sunbonnet.../...No, but it tore out
a lot of her hair.../...I know it's dark and airless and
uncomfortable...but I feel safe.../...as long as I'm
back of this old desk. An arrow couldn't go through
it.../...What do you think I brought it along for?
Certainly not its looks...It's an ugly old thing.
(SQUEAL.) George, turn that gun away! Please!
I don't care if it's not loaded. It might go off all

the same. Keep it turned *away*! George, when are we going to get there? And where is it we're going to *get*? I'm so tired, George.../...and I'm so tired of being tired. And I'm so tired of being tired of being tired. Nothing ever happens...and when it does, it's something awful...Oh dear! (PAUSE.) What is it now, George? Why are we stopping?... (RISING, STARING AHEAD, THEN WITH A SHRIEK, FALLING BACKWARDS, HANDS OVER EARS.) *Indians*!!! (SCREAMING AND COWERING UNDER THE DESK.)

- - - - - - - - - - -

Introduction - The Descendant, A Southern
            Lady Guide

> The setting is in one of those stately, historical mansions in Charleston, South Carolina which are open to the public -- for a stipend. Each has an ultra-refined lady guide in attendance. This one, a maiden lady of indeterminate years, is willowy, at times ecstatic and always painfully genteel. She speaks with an extreme Southern accent:

ONE WOMAN SHOW

NOW I RECKON THAT'S ALL THERE IS TO TELL YOU about the lovely little old Colonial garden so if you would step this way I'd be mighty glad to show you-all this lovely little old Colonial card room. I don't know if those folks yonder at the back can hear me plainly. Ha! I'm forever bein' teased about my liddy-biddy voice. In this part of the South we were all brought up to speak so soft and gentle...and of course this role of bein' a lady guide is a mite unusual one in our family. I think so often, what would my ancestors say could they know their sweet old mansion had been opened up as a sight-seeing place for visitors....visitors from the North! Oh I hope you-all will excuse me. I'm just so tactless! But I can't help my little old self. It's the way I was brought up. Why, would you actually believe that I was a young lady of fourteen before I knew that damn-Yankee wasn't one word? Ha-ha! But, of course I realize you-all are different because you're from Philadelphia and, I understand, Philadelphia's had some mighty lovely ancestors. Well this, as I mentioned before, is the little old card room where the family sat in the evenings. An' it's still furnished just like in those gracious days of the Cavaliers. Lady Ethelinda was such an elegant creature...She was born in London, England and my folks and I are directly descended from her and her dashin' husband Sir Fitz-James...

ONE WOMAN SHOW   Page 81

There's always been a Fitz-James in our family. Well, as I was saying, this is where Sir Fitz-James and Lady Ethelinda spent their evenings long ago. Can't you-all just picture how it was? The scent of magnolia wafting in from the garden, the note of the whippoor-will mingling with the singing of the slaves; Lord Fitz-James in this chair reading aloud a book of poetry to the exquisite Lady Ethelinda as she sat at this table doing her embroidery, so contented in her beautiful home in the new world.

Introduction - The Aristocratic Southern
            Ancestress

>   The performer sits at the table and attaches
>   a ringlet so it falls down over one shoulder,
>   adjusts her headpiece and goes through
>   the motions of playing solitaire. She is a
>   blowsy, common English woman from
>   Drury Lane Theatre with a cockney accent
>   --- Lady Ethelinda herself:

RED QUEEN ON BLACK KING. I had a knave hereabouts...what the devil's become of that knave?

Page 82 ONE WOMAN SHOW

Ach! Stuck underneath the ten! (FINGERS
TABLE.) Small wonder. Everything's sopping in
this climate. (PLAYS A BIT. SLAPS MOSQUITOES)
Drat the mosquitoes! Where's Sambo? He's supposed to stand by and shoo 'em away! It's taking
him the deuce of a time to fill your decanter of port.
(SLAP!) Meanwhile, ducky, your poor wifey's
being all et up by the monsters. I shall look a sight...
(SCRATCHES ARMS, BACK AND DOWN BOSOM.)
Acht! Three more cards stuck together! (GATHERS
UP PACK.) What's the use? I've played till I'm
squint-eyed. This filthy weather...everything sticks...
the cards stuck...the table drawers stuck...my clothes
stuck...Look, Fitzy, I'm fair glued to my bodice!
(FANS DOWN FRONT.) And, oh God! There goes
that ghastly bird again! (IMITATES WHIPPOOR-
WILL.) What an idiotic sound! Don't it make you
nervy, Fitz? It's all very well for you, Lord of the
Plantation...you great squire, you sprawling there
with your shirt open as wide as your mouth...snoring
louder than a smith's bellows. What with three
bottles of burgundy at dinner you can sleep through
the heat...and the blooming whippoorwill and all.
(SLAP.) Winged vermin! But may I? Lord love you,
no! Not the squire's lady! She must set an example
to the countryside....Her ladyship must stay home
of an evening, play patience, sew a fine seam and

ONE WOMAN SHOW

take an occasional sip of madeira. (RISES.) I think I'll have a bit of a sip right now. (WALKS WITH DIGNITY TO BACK.) Whippoorwill! Wouldn't you think the silly creature'd try a new tune now and then? (POURS WINE.) And oogh! That smell! That nauseous perfume! Close the window and you perish with the heat, open them and you get the stench of that eternal magnolia! (DRAINS GLASS.) Oh, to breathe the smells of dear old London just once again before I die of boredom! Remember the smell backstage at Drury Lane? You'd be standing there...waiting for me in the wings? And the smell of roast and ale and a cozy fire in our private room at the Goat and Beadle where you'd take me after the show, ducky? That was life! (REFILLING GLASS.) Little did I think when I finally got you to marry me, your wicked old pater'd ship you off to fester in this land of steaming heat, stinking trees, shrieking birds and (SLAP) flying cannibals! Fitzy-witzy, they're eating your poor Ethelinda alive...that they are! They're devouring her army-warmies and her bosomy-wosomy... Will nothing rouse you, you wine keg? (DRINK.) Heaven help us! As if that bird wasn't trial enough, the slaves have to start in their doleful singing! And it's night after night after night! Fitzy, can't you do something about it? No use talking to you. As well hold converse with a pickled corpse. (ENTER

SAMBO.) Oh Sambo. You're here at last. You brought his Lordship's port? I am about to retire for the night. After his Lordship wakes up and finishes the decanter, assist him upstairs, put him to bed and bring him his puke-basin. Go order the slaves to cease their singing and when you go, take along his Lordship's gun and shoot that bloody whippoorwill!

- - - - - - - - - - -

THE VANISHING RED MAN

*This is an impersonation of a clublady...
the Helen Hokinson type, who has been
spending some months on a reservation
in Arizona and has gone quite mad over
American Indians. I always played her
with an exaggerated Boston accent because somehow the absurd incongruity of
a Back Bay resident mingling with the
primitive Red Man seemed to me funnier
than having her come from some less
prim and proper locale. She is smilingly
pleasant, ecstatically dedicated and
generally idiotic. She should be played
in dead seriousness when she quotes
bits of Indian Philosophy and when she
goes into her "Wolf Dance" routine.
Since the list of props for this sketch
is quite extensive, they have been listed
at the end of the book.*

Introduction

This is an impersonation of a clublady
who has been spending some months
on a reservation in Arizona and has gone
quite mad over American Indians.

ONE WOMAN SHOW

(ENTERS WITH INDIAN PARAPHERNALIA.) OH THANK YOU, MARGARET. I think if I just put my things here I'll be perfectly fine.../...Oh, yes, I'll have plenty of room if Mrs. Perkins would just push her chair a little further --- and then, Margaret, if you don't mind pushing that rug back --- There! You know it's such fun to be back with you girls again. All the time I was in Arizona I thought so much about you and kept wishing you could share in my Indian adventure. However, as the old tribal sage remarked, "Dreams and smoke are not to be captured", so --- I am here today with a few of my treasures (INDICATING JUNK) to bring our luncheon group a glimpse of the West. As you know, I am just back from Arizona, where for six months it has been my privilege to have the privilege of....er....actually living with the Indians...Actually, that is, of course I had my own private teepee...I mean...I didn't go completely native...but...well, I did. I lived six months ...or in Navajo parlance, six times of the moon growing from a bow to a squash, with the Indians. I shared their birch tea and acorn mush, I smoked their calumets of kinnick-kinnick (although as you know, I don't ordinarily smoke cigars) and every night I slept on a bed of sweet sage with my feet to the east...which is Mojave medicine. Through the courtesy of our Senator Faffner who has so at heart

the cause of our Red Brother and who ... Oh, dear,
the Senator is a dear...who invented those stirring
words "America for the Americans." I had the entree
...or as the Shoshones say, "The right to go from
dampness walking into dryness sitting," to the Reservation. Because of my friendship with the Senator,
I do believe that bill is about to come up in the
Senate, they made me an honorary member of their
tribe. And that is why...(PUTTING ON REGALIA.)
...as a full-fledged tribal member I have the right to
wear this ceremonial garb...Ha! If you'll just wait a
moment I'm just going to show you -- Of course I'm
not wearing all of it...there is more...(INDICATING
BELOW THE WAIST.)...the ceremonial garb of the
...er...Mojave...er...maiden...of course, being the
mother of two boys at Harvard, you girls may smile
--- but it is what they gave me. The design is one that
came to the mighty warrior Sore-Foot in a dream. I
don't know if you can get the motif but it illustrates
a telling heard in the hogans of the Utes, the Paiutes
and the Haiutes. I have a pattern of this that I'd be
delighted if anybody'd like to copy it. I have also a
most practical war-bonnet pattern if you're interested
in war-bonnets. I know Lucy said something about
the Beaux Arts Ball and what on earth she'd put on
Elliot. This garb and the war-bonnet are only for
dress occasions. In fact, the war-bonnet is worn as

a sort of...well, a sort of tuxedo. And they are so
beautiful! How I wish our men would wear something as picturesque in the evenings. And let me show
you my moccasins. (PULLING UP SKIRT TO EX-
HIBIT THEM.) Honestly, girls, when you have tasted
the joy and freedom of the moccasin, you will say
"Ba-ku-ta," Manitou for "goodbye," to your heels
forever....Now in these few minutes that our group
allows, let me take you to the little Arapahoe village
ruled so wisely by that splendid old American chief,
Nick-wah-hoo (in our clumsy language Chief Many
Tail Feathers)...let me share with you my medicine
dream. Let me touch your moccasin with mine...Ha!
An old saying of the Chippewa. It all seemed indeed
the Happy Hunting Ground. Gay with the sound of
drums and eagle songs. The women with their
papooses going about women's business...the old men
dreaming over the peace or thunder-pipe and the
young braves...(GETTING QUITE COY.) Oh, dear
me! The young braves, acting as young braves will...
performing feats of strength and courage...and puri-
fying their lithe young bodies with smoke of sweet-
grass...of course, I never watched them doing that.
Ah, it was all perfectly marvelous! You'll be interested to know that my most faithful friend was
one of the young braves...(VERY COY.) Oh, a dear
boy! Named Oh-Hunka-Mo...meaning Bear-that-

ONE WOMAN SHOW   Page 89

Sings...His father before him, famous in the tribe, was
Bear-Going-Home....And his father's father -- I suppose
I should say his Grandfather --- was the famous Bear-
From-The-Waist-Down -- that is of course B-E-A-R. Oh,
I did so wish you all might have known this young
fellow...so muscular...so handsome...so anxious to
please...and at heart just as full of fun as a chipmunk.
Really it was just like knowing Hiawatha --- Hunka-Mo
had eaten the heart of the grizzly bear to obtain self-
mastery...he had also...and, oh, I think this little
Arapahoe custom is just darling...He had caught a
yellow butterfly and had rubbed its wings over his...
er...legs to assimilate the swiftness and grace of these
pretty creatures. He it was who took me to witness
the tribal dances and now, if Mrs. Perkins will just
move a little further over, I should like to picture for
you one of these dances. (GETS PROPS READY,
PUTTING DRUM ON CHAIR, ETC.) One morning
before Shau-Din...that's Dawn...my young friend came
to my hogan and waking me by shaking a gourd said,
"The wolves are approaching the Pueblo, O Woman.
Come with me and learn a wonder." He said, "O
Woman." But he didn't mean that. Hastily I pulled
about my shoulders the bright Navajo blanket. My
goodness! You'd have laughed if you'd seen me
dressed in a blanket instead of a wrapper! And I
came forth from my primitive little dwelling, my heart

ONE WOMAN SHOW

beating like a tom-tom. For I knew I was about to witness the famous *wolf dance.* To give you the proper atmosphere I should have a water-drum...and do you know my water-drum was shipped last week from the west and has not as yet arrived...I'm perfectly furious with the express company!...However, I can approximate the tempo on this smaller drum. Now this (PICKING UP DRUM, BEATING A SHORT RHYTHM) is what the drummers play before the entrance of the wolves. Those of us who are familiar with our Indian rhythms, I believe Miss Mason is, will recognize the plea for rain...which must be distinguished from...(REPEAT EXACTLY THE SAME RHYTHM.) ... which is the plea for the young corn. And this... (REPEATING THE SAME RHYTHM EXCEPT FOR A SLIGHT PAUSE BETWEEN TWO OF THE DRUM BEATS.) Ha! Do you hear that beat that isn't there? That is the plea for...er...fertile ...squaws. Then there enters a scout in wolf-attire who speaks the prologue...(PUTTING ON PINCE-NEZ AND PICKING UP THE PIECE OF BIRCH BARK.)....which, if you'll forgive me, I shall read because I am not sure of the words, and my eyes have gotten so bad I've just got to use glasses -- Lucy, I see you've come to them, too. He says... I've written it on birch-bark as being more in keeping ...he says...oh yes, and he intersperses the lines with

ONE WOMAN SHOW   Page 91

rattling a gourd. (PRODUCES A RATTLING GOURD.)
I did bring my gourd. You know I just couldn't bear
to part with it. I had it on the plane with me and I
can't tell you what interest it roused in the other
passengers...Well, to return to our scout, he said "Hai-
ya, hai-ya...Titu wah hoo." Ha! Perhaps I had better
read you this in Pale Face. He says Ho! Ho! Great is
the wisdom of the chickadee. (SHAKES GOURD.)
Great is the power of the Thunder pipe. (SHAKE.)
But greater still is Wolf who walks in the mountains.
(TAKING OFF PINCE-NEZ. SPEAKS IN REVER-
ENTIAL TONE.) ... There's a subtle philosophy in
that to my mind! Then enter the dancers. They
wear only a single wolfskin around their...loins...
It really was perfectly thrilling...the tail hanging down
in the...the characteristic place...(INDICATE BY
HANGING AN ARM OVER HER REAR, WAVING
IT.)...and here, here is the mask that they wear.
(PICKS UP MASK AND HOLDS IT OVER FACE.)
Now don't be afraid! You'd hardly know me, would
you? The wolves advance. (PANTOMIMES.) Bent
forward as if sniffing out a trail. (TAIL PANTO-
MIME.) The tails swaying in unison, they circle
about the fire. The squaws, meanwhile, form a
larger circle...they are of course larger than the men,
and stand as if harkening. (GESTURE OF HAND TO
EAR.)...The wolves lean forward and give a long, low

howl...which I would imitate except that...I'm afraid Margaret's servant might give notice. Ha! The drums then change to a more passionate tempo (LOOK FOR DRUM).../...It is the rhythm of growing things, of primitive ceremony and...if you'll pardon me, of mating. To this the wolves do a step that you will note is partly the stamp, partly heel-toe and partly the hop-step. (GOING INTO AN ENERGETIC DANCE WITH MUCH LEAPING AND STAMPING.) (SHOUTING.) Hai-ya! Hai-ya! ... The dancers leaping about like a pack gone mad...barking and howling...It was a regular orgy! Then suddenly the drums cease. The wolves form another circle, raise their heads and howl as if baying at the moon and the dance...er...ends. ... Oh, my goodness, I might go on indefinitely, but "No man can tell all" which is a saying of the Blackfeet. And besides I think I'm going a little over time...But I just want to say that after our bridge as a little surprise I'm going to have you taste some osage birch tea and some love-cakes made as the Zunis make them...of acorn flour. Ha! I thought that would be a pleasant surprise. And now, girls, in the words of the formula for leave-taking. (SALUTE. RAISES ARM, HAND FLAT, PALM OUTWARD.) "May the Spirit of Wakondah bless your hogans, and your corn ripen yearly" ... which is a saying of the Cherokees...Thank you very much.

- - - - - - - - - - -

A SUBSCRIBER TO THE SYMPHONY

This is written in the form of a train of thought. It represents what goes on in the mind of the average young married woman as she attends the Friday symphony concerts by herself. ... What distracts her, how her mind wanders off into various channels and how her attention keeps resolutely returning to the music which she is determined to appreciate. She sits in the chair with arms. There is no action except when she turns to stare at certain members of the audience or gives a little jump when a sudden sound from the orchestra recalls her to her "appreciation of music." The business of kicking off her shoes is optional. She can actually do it if retrieving them is not too awkward. I, myself, found it easier to imply it in pantomime. The only prop is a concert program.

Introduction

> This is in the form of a train of thought. It represents what goes on in the mind of a lady who attends the Friday afternoon symphony concert by herself.

ONE WOMAN SHOW

(GETTING INTO SEAT ... BREATHLESS.) JUST ON THE DOT! That's luck! Awful people who're late. Inexcusable to be late. Just got in myself before they closed the doors. (SETTLING DOWN.) Ah! This is civilized! The symphony...all to myself! Nobody to have to talk to. How delicious after all that shopping! Must be why my feet hurt so. I think I'll just kick off my shoes. Concentrate better on the music without my feet on my mind. Bet most of these women here can't concentrate. (CONDUCTOR ENTERS.) Ah! Here comes Mr. Grabowski. (APPLAUDING.) Oh I do admire him. Huh! As though every other woman in this audience didn't. Only with most of them it's because of his looks, not his conducting. Silly old hens. (SIGH.) He *is* goodlooking though. Not using a score -- there's musical scholarship! (LOOKS AROUND, ANNOYED.) Buzz! Buzz! Wish they'd quiet down so he could start! Oh-ho, no, not the concert, ladies. (VOCIFEROUS.) Sssssshhh! What is the matter with women? Look at them! Not one watching Mr. Grabowski! (TURNING AROUND HERSELF.) Look at old Mrs. Prendergast...staring up at the boxes...fanning her big front with her program! What does she think a program's for? Why doesn't she bring along a palm leaf fan? (STARTS FANNING SELF WITH PROGRAM.)

ONE WOMAN SHOW   Page 95

Oh! (REALIZES SHE IS DOING SO AND GLANCES
GUILTILY LEFT AND RIGHT. MUSIC STARTS.)
Heavens! It's begun. What's first? No, I'm not going
to look at the program because I bet I can tell. (HUM.)
Ha! Of course. Beethoven! Right from the start
you could tell. Nothing like Beethoven. Glad I joined
that music appreciation course. Know how to appreciate this. (EYES CLOSED AND HUMMING.)
Yes...yes. This is the *allegro*...that glorious opening
allegro...that glorious opening *allegro.* Or maybe it's
the *andante.* It's something at any rate. It's something. I've got the recording at home. It's what I
was playing the other night when Robert and I
started that silly, silly scrap...why he feels he has to
fuss when I turn on my classical records. (GOING
INTO DIALOGUE.)   It's simply an act with you,
Robert...and I don't mind saying a rather tiresome
one.../...Classical music isn't tiresome...you're just
being stubborn. You could learn to like it if you'd
only learn to like it.../...You may not want to but
Bobby should. I suppose you'd have his musical
education limited to rock and football songs. Well,
it may interest you to know, Robert, that a lot of
people you admire in this community are going in
for more cultural things than golf and the stock-
market. Even your little glamor wampus is in our
music appreciation group.../...Ha! As if you don't

know who I mean!.../...Oh Robert, it's too childish even to mention...only Peg McFadden's got a definite reputation and when you leave the country club dance with her and are gone over an hour...Of course I don't think anything. But I do think what people think...Not that that's *what* I think. (JUMP AT MUSIC.) Oh! This glorious Beethoven! As if I'd waste one second of it thinking about Peg McFadden! Too silly! If I ever started really thinking about Peg McFadden I'd...I'd...I wonder what I *would* think. I don't for a moment believe she and Robert even so much as...Of course she's capable of anything, but thank heaven Robert's not. He's merely capable of being the average man. Ach! What nonsense while there's this thrilling music. So pleased I'm getting to know my Beethoven. This is that familiar part that's so familiar. (SINGING.) Dya, dya, dee, da! Dya, dya dee da! That's the part with the bass violins. Wonder how you find out you've got a talent for the bass violin. Maybe Bobby has a talent for the bass violin. I'd rather he hadn't. (SINGING.) *1*, 2, 3, 4...1 and 2 and 3 and 4, 5, 6, 7, 8, 9, 10. (LOOKING UP AND COUNTING WITH FINGER.) That organ has an awful lot of pipes. (CRASH.) (JUMP.) Och! Mercy! The cymbals! And that little man in the back row who clashes them just once during the program. His one big moment.

ONE WOMAN SHOW　　　　Page 97

Except when he pings the triangle. Bet I could ping
a triangle. (HUM.) (HUM SOME MORE, THEN LOOK
AROUND.) Tch! How *can* people cough! Just shows
they're not listening. (SLIGHT COUGH.) These old
hens don't listen. They only come to the symphony
because it's the thing to do. Why would Miss
Twitchell come, for instance. She can't hear a note.
She's deaf as an adder. How do they know adders
are deaf? It's Mrs. Prendergast who's doing that
coughing! No wonder, she's got herself in a draft
the way she keeps fanning that upholstered old
bosom of hers. Bet she looks funny in a bra...bet
she looks funnier without one. Ooh! What a grue-
some thought! (SMILE QUIETLY.) I don't look
so bad in a bra. I don't look bad at all. I look kind
of young. Don't believe I ever saw Peg McFadden
in a bra. I'll bet she's obvious. Bet she wears
falsies. Ha! There'd be a disillusionment for her
collection of scalps. Not that Robert's one of her
scalps. He's merely amused by her. After all, last
summer I was amused...if that's what you want to
call it. (SMILE.) Wonder what he's doing these
days. Wonder if he thinks of me now and then.
(PAUSE.) I guess he does. The way I think of him
...now and then. (MUSIC.) And this is not going
to be one of the *nows*! Beethoven's too important.
(EYES CLOSED IN RAPTURE.) Nothing like

ONE WOMAN SHOW

Beethoven! There go the brasses. I mean the woodwinds...the things they blow on. You can tell which men are playing by their foreheads turning red. How unaesthetic! Especially that clarinet player who spreads that little piece of velvet over his knee. For catching the spit? Yach! And hasn't he a greasy face. The way he puffs out those shiny cheeks on every note. Wonder if he's married. Wonder if he puffs out his cheeks when he kisses his wife. I'd certainly hate to kiss him. I'd much rather kiss Mr. Grabowski. (SQUIRMING IN SUDDEN PANIC.) What if I did? What if I were suddenly to rush up onto the stage and *kiss* Mr. Grabowski! What if I went crazy and did! Better not think about it or I might! Wouldn't it be funny if I ever got to know him and *did* kiss him sometime. Be kind of... although I don't know about his moustache. Yet when you kiss a man with a moustache you don't really notice the moustache. Or do you? Let's see... there was that Englishman years ago. And that incident last summer had a moustache. Wonder how many nice women...because I'm a nice woman... I really am. I'm a nice woman...How many *have* incidents. How many in this audience, for instance. (LOOKING AROUND AT THEM.) Bet Mrs. Prendergast never had an incident...even when she was young. Bet she always undressed under her

ONE WOMAN SHOW Page 99

nightgown. Don't suppose Mr. Prendergast ever saw her any other way. Now what on earth would make me think of that! Put my mind back on Beethoven. What majesty! I must try to sort of fill myself with this beauty and take some of it back to Robert and Bobby. Bobby especially. Darling, precious, dreadful Bobby! Thirteen's such an awful age. So hard to tell what a kid's thinking. He seems so slap-happy and yet so vulnerable. I don't suppose any mother ever completely reaches through to her kids. Last night when the thunderstorm came and I went in to close his window...and found him crying into his pillow and I said, what is it, Bobby sweetheart? Were you having a nightmare? What's the matter, honey? Is it because you didn't make the team?.../...No? Something happen in school? Or here at home? Can't you tell Mom?.../...All right, dear. Here's some kleenex. Call me if you need me. Night's a strange time. Robert was very cute when I got back to bed...very understanding when I said, Bobby was crying, Robert. He wouldn't tell me why.../...I guess so. Growing pains. When do growing pains stop? For any of us?.../...Sure I have 'em. I have 'em a lot. But I'd never dream that you would, Robert. We know so little about what's going on inside the people we love.../...Yeah. Except love. I guess that's all we need to know.../...Dearest of

ONE WOMAN SHOW

course I'll kiss you...any hour of the night...or day too...and that's a test! Oh, this lovely music! (HUM.) Dya dya dee da. Maybe if I put my shoes back on I'll pay more attention to the music. There's the left one...dya dya dee da. Where's the right one? Where the hell's my shoe? (SQUIRMING WITH FOOT TO LOCATE SHOE.) It's gone under there. I'll get it after this movement; it's nearly the end of this movement anyway. Forget my shoe and listen to this heavenly music. Beethoven! Glorious Beethoven! Did he write this before or after he went deaf? See if the program says. Let's see. Beethoven??? My God! It's Brahms!

THE YEARLY AMERICAN INVASION

This piece may be shortened, if desired, by cutting some of the six characterizations of various types of American women tourists in Paris. They are seen at various places and times of day in cafes and, in one instance, strolling through the Ritz Bar. For them I contrived a hat which could be twisted into a variety of shapes for individual characterization. It was made of soft red velvet, flat, shaped in a cartwheel, gathered a little at the front where it slipped onto the head. Inside and across the opening was a short piece of grosgrain sewn to both sides. This held it steady and kept it from turning around. Attached to the outer rim were a few large hooks and eyes which I'd fasten or unfasten to give the hat a different appearance for each of the impersonations. The arrangement was tricky but effective and required hours of practice in order to manage it easily before an audience. A possible substitute is any soft, wide-brimmed felt hat. With the hat, the performer should carry a bag. Mine was a nondescript, shapeless one made of the same red velvet as the hat. There are short introductions to each impersonation,

ONE WOMAN SHOW

> *explaining the locale, type of person,*
> *etc. This gives one a chance to arrange*
> *the hat and move the chairs when needed.*

Introduction to the Series and to The Shopper

> Every summer the city of Paris is invaded
> by the American horde. It has been so
> ever since the days of the Second Empire
> when the Duc de Morny remarked, "All
> good Americans, when they die, go to
> Paris." That's especially true of American
> women. If you wander about this city at
> various times of the night and day, look-
> ing in on bistros, bars and pavement cafes,
> you will find them at their most typical.
> Any one of these Parisian sketches will
> serve admirably if a short encore is de-
> sired. Let us begin with the noon hour
> at the Cafe de la Paix, or, as this lady
> from Brooklyn might call it, "The Cuffay
> dulla Pay." I played her with a Brooklyn
> accent because it sounded funnier and I
> wore the hat hooked up at a jaunty angle
> to imply an overly smart creation. Here
> is The Shopper. She is speaking to a
> friend:

SO I SAID TO THE SALES GIRL, "I'll take three
bottles of the Chanel and eight of the Shocking."
I'd already purchased the Guerlain.../...No, I planned

ONE WOMAN SHOW

to hide them in my handbag. But you know how conscientious Arthur is and very, very ethical about exhibiting all our bills at the Customs. Of course we always have them made out for less than we paid -- that's only logical. Every woman appreciates a gift of Paris Parfum and when they know you've been abroad they expect it.../...You know, dear, what Mrs. Corbus is doing about her gifts? She's using wrapping paper from Saks Fifth Avenue and from Bonwit's so the recipients will think they cost a lot more.../...Ha ha ha! She thinks she's so clever, but I think they'll catch on!...No, go ahead, dear. Tell me about Monte Carlo. We intended to go there but we went to Rome instead, and in certain respects I regret it. Oh, Rome was very, very interesting -- all those ruins. They were thoroughly enjoyable and in a certain restaurant we sat near Gina Lollobrigida! That was outstanding. But you know, dear, in Italy all the food is Italian and Arthur complains it gives him heartburn. And then I was very, very desirous to return to Paris. To me, Paris is gorgeous. Arthur prefers the Poconos but I always say Paris is gorgeous. Oh, Arthur appreciates the entertainment. We saw the show at the Follies "Perchere" (meaning Bergeres), but Arthur was disappointed. They've cleaned it up a lot. Men are so gross. Now go on dear, tell me all about Monte Carlo.

- - - - - - - - - - -

Page 104   ONE WOMAN SHOW

Introduction to the Debutante

> Paris would probably still be Paris without
> the presence of the Ritz Bar, although it
> might not seem so to the faithful habitues
> of that place, especially to the very young,
> the very rich and the very socially-registered.
> The debutante is one of these. She is typi-
> cal of the East Coast social set and talks
> with that lackadaisical drawl that I like to
> call Park Avenue lock-jaw. Her frequent
> "it's too, too divine" is said with no vestige
> of enthusiasm. Her blank expression reveals
> a blank mind.

OH, COME ON, JEFF! OH, HOW TOO AWFUL!
There's no table but absolutely none! Oh hello,
Dewit and Nina, how divine to see you. How was
Antibe? I hear you saw the Windsors....Wasn't that
divine? Come on, Jeff. I think we'll find a place
over near the bar ... Oh, Mr. and Mrs. Chandler!
How divine to see you! You know my fiancé, don't
you? Um, I thought you might have met at my
debut party ... Oh, hello, Brenda! I haven't seen
you since Nassau. You're looking divine ... Mrs.
Chandler, I hope you and Mr. Chandler can come to
our wedding ... October first ... /... No, we're having
it in Oyster Bay. I hope it doesn't rain.../...Oh, yes,

I am! I'm absolutely thrilled. I'm getting all my
trousseau here in Paris. Schiaparelli's making my
wedding gown -- it's going to be absolutely divine.
Mummy was talking about having hers made over
but, Mrs. Chandler, Mummy was married in 1937.
The styles were absolutely ungodly! ... Oh, hello,
hello, Darcy! How'd you like the races?.../...No, I
only lost about five hundred francs ... Mrs. Chandler,
Mummy's going to be in Paris next week and I know
she'll want to see you. She and my stepfather are
off in Deauville. She says it's divine ... You know
Daddy's abroad, too. I suppose you heard he just
got married? She's awfully nice. They're having
their honeymoon ahead of ours. Isn't it divine? ...
Well, I know she'll want to see you. Goodbye, Mrs.
Chandler. Goodbye, Mr. Chandler. Come on, Jeff.
I mean I'll absolutely die if I don't get a champagne
cocktail!

Introduction to the Gourmet

> On the Left Bank, over near the Quai des
> Grands Augustina, is a small cafe where
> you get a good view of the western facade
> of Notre Dame. At about four in the after-
> noon you might come across this couple.

Page 106   ONE WOMAN SHOW

> The woman is dreadful. Why she and her
> husband, who is at the table with her,
> ever came to Paris is a mystery to whoever
> encounters her and to her too. She hates
> everything ... hates Paris, hates the food,
> hates the French. She longs only for a
> "good cup of Amerrr'c'n cawfee." She
> is glum, grim and her mouth is turned
> down at the corners in a perpetual grimace
> of distaste. For her I rolled up the brim
> of the hat into an uncompromising toque
> worn straight on the top of my head. She
> speaks:

HUH, UH-UH! NO, THERE'S ONLY ONE THING
I WANT. THAT'S A CUP OF COFFEE. I mean
real coffee. This stuff isn't coffee ... This stuff's
terrible. Always thought these people were so famous for their food. They certainly don't know anything about coffee. (WAVING AWAY WAITER.)
.../...No, no! I don't want your coffee! Your
coffee's terrible! I'll take -- oh, I don't know -- do
you have Coca-Cola? No use ... You can't get any
coffee. Huh, these French policemen kill me the
way they wave those white sticks around! Why do
they want to have them white?.../...Just four o'clock.
Can you imagine that? Just the time of day I like
a good cup of coffee.../...Oh, no, might as well sit

ONE WOMAN SHOW   Page 107

here -- there's nothing else to do.../...Neither do I. I don't know why *anybody* comes here.../...Evenings aren't so bad...Mornings you can sleep most of the morning. That helps pass the time.../...Tonight? I don't know. Might look in on that movie house up near the Arch where they show the American films. We'll see. ... There's that same woman selling those same tired old roses. Can you imagine anybody buying a cheesy little corsage like that?.../...No, no, go 'way -- they're terrible! Listen, we're from Fresno, California. Go 'way! ... Some sucker'll buy one ... You get a good view of Notre Dame from here. Gee, it sure is old, all right. Old and dirty. Wouldn't you think they'd clean it up? Aw, I don't mind that much. What really burns me is that you simply can't get a decent cup of coffee!

- - - - - - - - - - -

Introduction to the Art Student

> The Left Bank has always attracted the artistically dedicated. So, predictably, the Art Student will be found at the art students' hangout there, the Cafe Flore. She is a young thing dedicated to art, as

Page 108 ONE WOMAN SHOW

> she shows by the way she walks and talks.
> Her husky voice denotes chain smoking
> and late hours. She is determined to be
> f ⋅e and is aggressively Bohemian. The
> hat should be worn like an artist's Vie de
> Boheme beret pulled down loose over
> one ear.

HELLO, MAX, DID YOU GET YOUR CHECK FROM HOME YET? Huh! Good thing you finally shacked up with Nedda. (THEY ASK HER TO SIT AND SHE PLOPS DOWN DELIBERATELY STRADDLING THE CHAIR AND LEANING HER ARMS ON THE BACK.) Okay, are you going to have room for Tony? I told him he had to get out and get some air ... even if it was hot air. Oh, he's working himself anemic over this magazine cover commission. It was four in the morning before I could get him to bed. ... He wants to finish it so he can do some real painting. Oh, this commercial stuff is terrible for his conscience. (LAUGHING.) Listen, Max, this is one canvas that Tony's not going to allow anybody to see except two million readers of a bourgeois magazine.../...Stinks? Sure it stinks! It stinks as bad as Maxfield Parrish. .../...Sweetheart, how else are we going to pay the rent on the studio? It's unavoidable prostitution. ... I'll have my usual pernod. Well, what have I

ONE WOMAN SHOW

interrupted?.../...Oh, Stefan -- well, what *is* your concept of modern?.../...I'll tell you what's modern. We're modern! Leo, Stefan, Sonya, Max and Tony's modern too when he's not sacrificing himself for money! Listen, Tony's so modern that he even dares to be old-fashioned. Tony's so modern that only last week he suggested we get married! (LAUGHING.).../...No, of course not. We've got the studio. Why should we bother to get married?

- - - - - - - - - -

Introduction to the Correspondent

> Eventually every American gets up to the high summit of Montmartre and sits at one of the lamplit tables in the Place du Terte. This American is not a tourist. She's been living in Paris and has had a job since the war. Once attractive and talented, she is now slowly killing herself with drink. To indicate to what a degree her morale has sunk, I used to twist the hat into a nondescript form and mess up my hair into a few sloppy wisps. (She chuckles drunkenly.)

ONE WOMAN SHOW

I LAUGH, I JUST HAVE TO LAUGH...All this talk about his wife coming over! Order me another brandy ... You're cute, George. I thought you were cute ever since I came overseas and you were on the staff. You were smart, George, to get the hell out of the army. Did you know except for one little bitty trip home that I've been here since V-E Day? Could you believe a gal could be such a fool over such an ordinary forty-eight-year-old man, even if he is a general? Without his uniform he's just an ordinary guy pushing fifty! ... George -- George, listen. I -- I want to tell you something. I want to tell *you* something. Back home in Kentucky there's a guy, and he's crazy about me! He wants to marry me. And he knows all about this and he still wants to marry me. ... And he's a wonderful guy ... and I stay on in Paris, baking my own humble pie and eating it. George, do you know what happens next week? I stay in Paris and run the office while he goes on leave to Biarritz to meet his wife.../...Uh-uh. ... That's not his wife he's meeting. He's meeting a French gal.../...I know 'cause I opened a wire she sent him. So -- so he's meeting this gal and what am I going to do about it? (TRYING TO SNAP FINGERS.) And what do I care? (INEFFECTUAL SNAP.) Damn finger won't snap. ... George -- George, I think I'm a little --

little tight tonight. I -- I'm not getting to be any
alcoholic but I've been drinking too much lately.
And I don't like to drink. ... George, I don't like to
drink!.../...George, you're cute. ... George, I want to
tell you something. Did you know that back home
there's a guy who's crazy about me and wants to
marry me? He never did want me to join the WACS.
He wanted me to stay in Kentucky and marry him.
...But I wanted to be a war correspondent. Like a
lot of people, I was looking -- for something. You
don't think it was love of Uncle Sam? There was a
whole lot of them like me. They were in love with
something they never found. (CRYING.) It's not
that I'm jealous of her. I'm just so damned mad!
I've given that two-timer ten of the best years of
my life! Oh, he's done it before. ... But I'm not
as young as I used to be. I'm starting to lose my
looks. ... I don't reckon this is helping them any...
Oh, hell! I'll go fix my face. You get them to
hurry up with that brandy, George. ... You're cute,
George!

ONE WOMAN SHOW

Introduction to The Lovers

> And because Paris has been called
> 'The City of Lovers' there are lovers
> here. These two have met again, after
> years, not to find the magic gone and
> the music silent, but to find the magic
> more overwhelming and the music even
> sweeter. The children's carousels in
> the Champs Elysees are put away for the
> night and a few more stars are begin-
> ning to show through the thick foliage
> of the chestnut trees. At the Cafe du
> Rond Point, a man and a woman are
> finishing their drinks.

NO, DARLING, NO MORE FOR ME EITHER.
(TURNS HER WRIST.) I've got just a quarter of
.../.../Yes, dearest. You'd better allow a full hour
to the airport.../...No, I've my ticket straight through
to Zurich tomorrow night.../...Darling, I have to go.
I've been gone over a week and you know he gets
.../...The doctor says he mustn't be upset emotion-
ally ... Anyway, Paris without you -- twenty-four
hours are all I could stand.../...Of course.../...you
write me, too. Better General Delivery.../...Oh,
I don't know. We may stay in Switzerland.

We may go back to the States ... I don't know what
he'll want to do. ... You don't know her plans
either.../...No, that's not quite how it was. We didn't
get a second chance and refuse it again; we didn't
always let other people stand in the way -- your
family or my family, and we weren't always cheated.
We did see each other again. We thought it was all
gone -- but it wasn't and we had this whole marvelous week together here in Paris. A week ago and
I'd have settled just to see you across the street! I
wish to God I wasn't going back to that room tonight
.../...Oh, Darling, you've got to go .... Don't forget
your briefcase. Listen -- that sound?.../...No, it's
not rain. It's that funny night wind in the dry
leaves of the chestnut trees ... Darling, you've got
to go.../...Come, my love ... my love ...

- - - - - - - - - - -

Introduction to the American Wife

> And our final glimpse is of a plain, every-
> day couple from a plain everyday town.
> They are doing Europe on a budget. To-
> night they've splurged on one big gastro-
> nomic spree at a small but rather expensive

Page 114 ONE WOMAN SHOW

> restaurant up near the Etoile. She is a
> genuine dear, warm, intelligent and per-
> ceptive. This is her first trip abroad and
> she is loving every minute of it. She
> adores John, her husband, and feels that
> theirs is a wonderfully happy marriage.
> Her accent is mildly Middle-Western, but
> not offensively so. For this sketch I used
> to take a veil from the hand bag and tie
> it around the hat and down across my
> forehead. (Optional)

OH, JOHN, THE DINNER WAS PERFECT! Everything from the moules mariniere to the fraises de bois -- du bois -- des bois -- those little strawberries that taste like spring flowers ... Oh, there's still a drop of champagne left in my glass.../...Oh, honey, a pint was just perfect with that meal.../...Why, John, you're crazy. Brandy costs eight francs here -- that's more than a dollar ... I'll tell you what we could do though. Instead of taking a taxi home we could walk ... Stop in at that little bistro near the hotel.../...Okay, let's -- it's a lovely night for walking. ... Oh, first I want to thank that nice waiter. Oh -- oh, garçon! Garçon, uh, c'etait delicieux. Uh, nous sommes de Ohio et le diner etait a real treat. (LAUGHS.) He got it. ... Wait'll I go home and show off my French to Sonny. ... You know, a

few more years and he may be coming over. /...Oh,
work his way, or something.../...Won't he though?
No more of a kick than we've gotten though, huh?
John, I don't know -- maybe it's the dinner, or that
pint of champagne, but when I think that you and
I've been planning this trip since -- yeah -- since we
were first engaged -- and now to have it turn out
(SIGHS.) -- oh, golly, we're lucky! ... Are you ready?
(RISE AND STROLL.) Oh, what a beautiful night!
Don't you just love the way Paris smells? Smell!
Trees, taxicabs, tobacco smoke, perfume, flowers.
A little horse manure... (STOP WALKING. A
LITTLE GASP AND STARE IN AWE.) ... Oh, look!
Look, John! The Arc de Triomphe -- and the light
over the Unknown Soldier! That flame never goes
out no matter what happens. ... Year in and year
out it keeps on burning. ... Oh, gosh, I -- I'm just
crazy about this city! And I'm just crazy about you!
And isn't it nice that you're crazy about me?

- - - - - - - - - - -

MINUTEMAN'S WIFE

This sketch is best done over radio; sound effects will be more impressive: the horse's hoofbeats, the fife and drum corps at the finish. Besides, it might be physically awkward to give the impression that the woman is sleeping in a double bed with her husband. However if the performer can work it out for a stage performance, so much the better.

Introduction

Here we have a middle-aged, no-nonsense, early New England settler as she may have appeared on a certain well-known historic occasion.

WHAT'S THE MATTER WITH YOU, JONATHAN? Can't you stay still? You've bin turning and turning all night like a roasting chicken on a spit.../...'tisn't time to get up yet.../...That rooster crows any old durn time of the night. I tell you 'tisn't anywhere near dawn. I'll lay my life to it, 'tisn't any more'n two o'clock.../...Well, just because you're restless is no reason I should be kept awake...Lord a mercy, Jonathan, sleeping with you's like sleeping with a

ONE WOMAN SHOW   Page 117

colt.../...You were dreaming the British were coming?
....Well, you dream somethin' else.. Dream 'bout that
field you've got to plow tomorrow. That field ought
to 'uv bin ploughed two weeks ago...'t would uv bin
too if all you men hadn't gotten this Gub Dumb
foolishness forming that crazy Minute Man Brigade.
What you men who ought to be lookin' after your
farms want to waste a lot of time on makin' fools
of yourselves over this crazy talk about the British is
more'n a sensible woman can fathom... They aren't
comin' to Boston.../...No, nor to Concord, nor to
Lexington neither, nor to Bunker Hill, nor anywheres
else. You go to sleep, Jonathan...Forget the British
and think a little more about this summer's corn../..
Well, make up your mind...Which side d'you want
to lie on?.../...Very well, turn on your right side and
stay on it. (SIGH.).../...I didn't touch your gun...
It's standin' right where you left it leanin' against
the cupboard...I don't see why you want to keep a
gun in the bedroom.. It makes me nervous...puts
too many notions into my head...especially when
you keep me awake with your thrashing.../...Ready
for what?.../...Up and join the boys for defense?
(CACKLE.) I vow you men are no more'n a pack
of boys playin' soldiers. Go to sleep! Your rifle's
there an' that peddler's outfit you call your uniform's
on the chair beside it... Go to sleep now. I'll call

ONE WOMAN SHOW

you if the British need you. (HALF TO SELF.) I declare, you've got me wide awake and a-dither with all your palaver. (PAUSE.) Jonathan. You asleep? .../...No, you ain't.../...Well, not now, you ain't. Did you shut up the filly in the stall?.../...You sure?... Nothin'. I thought I hear a horse gallopin'...that's all. You know that time she got out she was half way to Hingham when they stopped her.. You sure you shut the barn door?.. Guess it wa'n't anything. Let's try the left side... You got me jumpin' now. (PAUSE.) Listen! That's her../.. the filly. That's her whinnyin'...She's in the barn all right. Wonder what's makin' her whinny like that? Must smell another horse.../...Well, go to sleep. Lands above, you've kept me awake half the night.. It's your turn to see how you like it. (PAUSE.) Listen! (PAUSE.) There *is* a horse gallopin' somewheres. (PAUSE. THE SOUND OF HOOFBEATS VERY FAINT.) Hear that?.../...Must be one o' Perkins' horses got loose again... That bay stallion o' his jumps plum over that fence he put up last month.. It's probably the stallion. (PAUSE.) He's comin' like Satan was on his tail. (HOOFBEATS SOUND NEARER.) Wonder if we oughta try an' head 'im off?.../... I don't warm much to Brother Perkins but someday the filly might get over his way.../...All right, you go on sleepin' if you want. I'm goin' to open the

ONE WOMAN SHOW   Page 119

shutters an' see if 'tus that stallion. (SOUND OF
SHUTTERS.) There's a moon so's you ought to be
able to see.. (LOUDER AND LOUDER HOOFBEATS.)
There's some lights over by the Green.../...Must be
some rowdies at the Old Mill Tavern settin' up a
bonfire.../...That horse is headin' right this way down
the road.. I kin see him now.. 'T ain't Perkins' stallion
...It's got a rider on 'im.. Now what crazy fool wants
to be ridin' at that speed at two in the morning?
He'll break his neck.. serve him right too... Too
many wild young men speedin' their horses on the
road... There should be a law 'bout it... He's slowin'
down now.../...that's good... Look! He's reinin' in.
He's reinin' in right spang in front of our yard...
(CALLING OUT.) What d'you want? Yes, this is
his house...Who wants 'im?.../... He's in bed.../...Just
who d'you think you are, young man, rousin' people
up this time o' night an' givin' 'em orders like you
was General Cornwallis?.../...Well, I don't know as I
will. Wait a second. It's that crazy boy of old man
Revere's...the one makes the silver...Paul...says he
wants to speak to you. Heavens! Jonathan! You
needn't leap out like the house was afire...most likely
he's drunk.../...Here he comes.../...How's that? The
British? Paul Revere, have you bin drinkin' over to
The Old Mill? Who told you?.../...You come all the
way from Boston? Yes, he's gettin' ready. Which

ONE WOMAN SHOW

way they comin', he says...by land or by the harbor?
.../...Both? He says they're comin' both ways. I
guess he's right... He talks sober enough... Where do
you want Jonathan?.../...He says the Green....that's
what all them lights are... Listen, young man Revere!
(GALLOPING HOOFBEATS FADING OUT INTO
THE DISTANCE.) He's gone already... says he's got
to rouse the boys at Lexington... That horse o' his
is half dead already...got more foam on it than the
roof had snow last winter.. Here, Jonathan... What
are you thinkin' of gettin' dressed in the dark....
Where's the tinder box?.../...Wait, you can't half
see... You'll be puttin' your arms through your pants
an' tryin' to step into your jacket.. (STRIKING
FLINT.) Lord! That boy's given me such a scare
I can't make this flint strike for nothin'. Crazy
fellow ridin' all over the map like a witch on a
Sabbath... He's mad anyway...any man that makes
silver instead o' takin' a hand at the farm same as
any decent patriot... Shouldn't wonder if he's
trumped up the whole notion about the British
outa that queezy head o' his. Now there's the
tinder lit an' here's a candle. Lord, Jonathan,
blessed if you ain't dressed already! Well, that's
something this drillin's taught you at any rate...
to dress quick. You ain't half got your shoes on.
Now wait, Jonathan, you can't go without somethin'

to eat...I'll rouse Sarah and we'll make you.../... You
ain't goin' out without somethin' inside you? This
April weather's colder'n it seems.../... Well, wait, I'll
git you a heel of bread and fill your canteen 'tany
rate.../...Oh it's full, is it? I wondered where that
port had disappeared to.../...Let me git you the
bread.../...Jonathan, you're stark mad! Who's goin'
to feed you, King George the Third? (DOOR SLAMS.)
Well, I'll be blest! (OPENING WINDOW.) Goodbye,
Jonathan! Now don't you go gittin' yourself shot at!
Remember you got that field to plow! When'll you
git back?...(HE GOES.) Of all the addle-pated things
to do to go to fight the British without somethin'
inside 'im! I don't know what's got into these men!
Looks like the person's goin' to plough that field is
me.... Well, we can't all be Minute Men! (CACKLE.)
Jonathan did look real handsome when he got fixed
up...(TOWARD THE FINISH ONE HEARS THE
SOUNDS OF A DISTANT FIFE AND DRUM CORPS
PLAYING "THE GIRL I LEFT BEHIND ME.")

- - - - - - - - - -

APPENDIX

Stage Properties for THE VANISHING RED MAN

This number requires a good many props, all of which must be put on before the audience with the exception of a pair of horn-rimmed pince-nez worn at the end of a long ribbon about the neck and a pair of Indian moccasins which should be kept as unobtrusive as possible until the moment when the performer deliberately exhibits them to view. The following items should be carried on and deposited on the table until time to put them on.

1. A knee-length Indian garment, sleeveless and open down the front. This can be faked out of one of those fringed suede or leather coats young people occasionally go in for. Indian symbols can be painted on it. Or the effect might be achieved with a coarse cotton material like canvas.

2. A few strands of beads; any sort as long as they suggest Indian beads.

3. A headband to be worn across the forehead. I happened to have a genuine beaded Navajo one, but the same impression could

be given with ribbons or braided vari-colored
woolen strands.

4. An eagle feather, or any feather that, at a
distance, will pass for one. It should be stuck
in the headband at the back.

5. A small drum like an Indian tom-tom, the
sort sold in Western souvenir shops, and a
primitive-looking wooden drumstick to beat
it with.

6. A flat piece of birch-bark large enough to
have writing on it.

7. A savage-like mask to be held before the
face during the "Wolf Dance." I was fortunate enough to find in a junk shop a Mexican
festival mask which served the purpose. It
was wooden, had fierce glaring eyes and
great outer tusks. Even one of those so-called
"African" masks which are frankly manufactured in this country, if painted up with
wild war-paint, will do nicely. It should,
however, be large enough to completely conceal the entire face.

8. A small gourd containing rattling seeds.
The sort used by dance orchestras when playing South American tunes.

Hand Props for LADY EXPLORER

Hand props to be used in presentation of LADY EXPLORER and detailed suggestion as to procedure to be followed in their use.

1. A metallic cricket. This is a small metallic device with which the performer signals the production man (at rear of hall) for a change of slides. Frequently she has to click it several times as he doesn't hear or simply couldn't care less.

2. A long, beaded chiffon scarf which she carries and puts on during the introduction. The scarf is brightly colored. It consists of two scarves, sewn together. It is placed about her shoulders and down her arms. It is shapeless.

3. Four or five long strings of heavy, arty beads. These are essential as she should have fun getting all tangled up in them toward the finish of the act. On one of these chains hangs a lorgnette which she uses to identify the slides and to refer to her notes.

4. A handful of cards with pencilled notations. The cards can get further mixed up to add to her confusion.

The business of getting all fouled up in the beads
should be carefully worked out and rehearsed.
Decide which string should fall over an arm so
that gestures swing them about and get them
caught about the throat. The funniest effect
for the exit is when one string of beads slips
down and hangs provocatively about the bottom
of the performer's rear, providing a sort of
"Beatrice Lillie" exit.

Notes

Notes

Notes

Notes

Notes